VOLUME 13   OUT-PAR

THE PRACTICAL ENCYCLOPEDIA OF

Good Decorating
and Home Improvement

GREYSTONE PRESS

Alphabetically arranged and fully illustrated, your *Practical Encyclopedia of Good Decorating and Home Improvement* has been planned for your convenience and immediate use. In feature articles you will find a wealth of facts, ideas, suggestions, and advice that will help you solve your decorating problems. A Master/Guide at the back of each volume includes concise articles of historical interest, definitions of terms, and summaries of feature articles in the volume. Helpful cross-references appear throughout all volumes. On many pages you will find illustrations and descriptions of Project Plans and Home Plans, identified by the abbreviations **PP** and **HP**. For information on ordering these plans write to Good Decorating Plans Editor, Greystone Press, 225 Park Avenue South, New York, N.Y. 10003.

A Practical Guide for Parties
By Daylight or Moonlight

One of fine weather's greatest joys is that you can share Nature's delights with your family and friends. When the weather is just right, any excuse to have a party outdoors—either under the sun or under the stars—is a good one.

All you need for your potential party room is a tiny balcony or minute patch of grass—although a backyard or terrace or patio will give you more opportunity to do things in the grand manner. But the only requirements are fresh air and a view, with perhaps some food and drink to nourish a sense of well-being.

What should you celebrate out-of-doors? A birthday or the Fourth of July make fine occasions. But the deciding factor is, of course, the weather. Another important consideration is your family's summertime activities. If your children swim or play tennis, encourage them to invite their friends home afterward for soft drinks and sandwiches.

Doors slide open onto a mini-terrace, where the party fare is grilled over a hot charcoal fire. At the other end a portable bar has been set up. Guests can dine inside or out. Special garden lighting sets a properly festive mood.

Sliding glass doors make this balcony almost a part of the living room. Wall sconces hold candles for romantic evening dining, while awning protects guests from the weather.

Planning

As with any kind of entertaining except the most impromptu, planning is the most important ingredient for the success of your outdoor parties. For example, some outdoor furniture is squirmingly uncomfortable. If you entertain in the open frequently, make certain that your chairs are ones in which it is easy to relax. If you use folding metal chairs, provide them with cushions. Be certain that your table or tables and your serving board are sufficiently large to accommodate the number of guests you have invited.

If your outdoor party is not to be served buffet-style, set your table (or tables) as carefully as you would for any indoor entertainment. However, an outdoor party calls for—even demands—gaiety and casualness. So set your table with colorful mats, dishes, and napkins.

Before your guests arrive, spray the party area with a mild insect repellent. (Strong insecticides are not consistent with either hospitality or, in some cases, with accepted ecological principles.) Scented candles are attractive and relatively effective repellents.

Locales

Almost any reasonably secluded area adjacent to your home provides a perfectly adequate setting for outdoor entertaining. The backyard is a natural, particularly if you have a lawn bordered by flower beds. A patio or terrace will also serve beautifully as a setting for your parties. Balconies and gazebos are also excellent places in which to entertain your guests outdoors. Even a nearby park, meadow, or inviting stand of trees can provide a picnic spot.

Part of the house shown below is seen in detail at right. ▶ The roof is beams, in three sections, each one covered in translucent plastic roofing. Behind the game and dining table, a base cabinet holds a small sink; above it, the cabinet contains storage for dishes. The full-length closet alongside it provides storage space for furniture throughout the winter. The low serving platform to the left of the table is ingenious camouflage for a large tree stump.

The small redwood house below, tucked away in a garden, combines all the joys of summer shade or summer sun into one compact structure. The floor of the garden house extends to form a curving plank patio.

Helpful hints

In addition to good food, quenching drinks, and pleasant company (standard requirements for any party), entertaining out-of-doors demands a few extras. First, you must forget the old saw that says outdoor entertaining is easier. Instead, plan your party in terms of graciousness rather than in terms of your personal convenience.

For example, make certain that you have enough chairs for each of your guests to sit both comfortably and gracefully. If you prefer a degree of formality, even outdoors, use heavy linen napkins instead of paper ones. Set your bar and table with sturdy glasses. To give your party a country look, and at the same time retain dining-room comfort, use pottery instead of paper plates. Be certain it is hefty and durable. Keep food hot with an electric warmer, or at least use metal covers on your hot dishes.

If you are entertaining outdoors during the evening, provide soft lighting for your party area. Candles under glass take over the lighting chore beautifully just as the sunset fades away.

Most important, have the good sense to plan to take your party indoors if the weather or the wind or insects become too bothersome.

Food for cook-in-eat-out parties is less likely to cool between oven and table if the table is on a nearby terrace rather than on the lawn. Your terrace can be planted and decorated to look as though it forms part of your garden. If you are serving a cold meal, your picnic plans can be more flexible, since less time and equipment are involved, and the picnic spot need not be located near the house.

Modern backyard swings can also easily take a turn as seats for a luncheon underneath the trees. Whimsical as these swings—and the lounging chairs beyond—may appear, each one is comfortably contoured to the relaxed human form. The furniture is made of rust-resistant frames wrapped with weatherproof vinyl-coated rattan.

Roughhewn boards, laid horizontally, form a simple, yet elegant, backdrop for outdoor entertaining on the small terrace of a city apartment, above. The wall provides privacy, furnishes support for climbing vines, and serves as a graphic-art gallery. The small roof shades only the dining area, leaving space open to the sky.

A narrow porch, right, has been skillfully turned into a ▶ beautiful setting for outdoor dining. The white-painted brick walls add apparent space to the area, and the plank-board floors lend rusticity and naturalness. A profusion of growing plants in clay pots completes the decorating scheme. The white chest provides extra storage space.

Stylish picnics

A picnic can be tossed together in 15 minutes —and look it—or it can be prepared with extra planning and care and thus come off as a thoroughly beautiful outdoor party.

Dining alfresco was without question practiced by the cavemen. Since then, classical and Renaissance art are full of idyllic depictions of picnics on the meadows, complete with fine linen, elaborately served courses, crystal goblets, musicians, and pretty serving maids.

Twentieth-century picnics may be simpler, but they need not be less picturesque. Consider a picnic of country fare eaten from a patchwork quilt spread on an open meadow in the shade of stately trees. The food includes hearty sandwiches, fresh raw vegetables, breads and cheeses, and a bottle of wine. Or a tailgate

◄ Main course for a hearty yet simple lunch on the beach, left, is fried and chilled chicken drumsticks, accompanied by a hot baked bean casserole. The beans can be kept piping hot in an insulated bucket. A variety of sauces, dips, and relishes to garnish the chicken can be provided in plastic cups. Hot rolls with plenty of butter go hand-in-hand with the chicken.

Why not turn an outing into your own classical picnic by serving gourmet fare, as below, in a romantic setting? A cooling and easy-to-prepare luncheon consists of vichyssoise, marinated cold steak, and sparkling Burgundy, all of it portable in one wicker basket and an ice chest. For dessert, serve chilled grapes and two kinds of cheeses. Crystal wineglasses add an extra touch of elegance.

buffet served from your station wagon and eaten on nearby tree stumps, rocks, and grassy knolls. Or a bicycle-basket picnic featuring sandwiches, salads in plastic tubs, fruit, cheese, and cold beer.

To make your picnic look like a party or festive occasion, pack each course in color-matched bags and boxes; then tie the boxes with bright contrasting yarn. Use linen cloths and napkins instead of paper ones, and serve all beverages from china or crystal.

Porch dining

Whether the family gathers for a summer sunrise breakfast or friends join you for a gourmet dinner for six, the best of the beautiful outdoor world is often your own practical porch or terrace. Just across the threshold from your house or apartment, the outdoors is often as handy to the kitchen as is the dining room; you can easily run back for seconds from the warming oven and feel confident that the food will stay hot till it reaches the table.

It is obviously not necessary to cook indoors. A broad choice of equipment is available for alfresco cooking. Your preference and your menu will dictate whether to use a larger grill (manual or electrified spit), hibachi, or an electric skillet. Surrounded by your own particular view of summer—a garden, a country wood, the sea, or even the glittering city at night—it can take your spirit miles from home.

To make certain that your porch is an adequate party room, scale each gathering to size. Have enough tables and chairs to accommodate everybody—and make certain they are every bit as comfortable as your indoor dining chairs. Never skimp on the comforts of china or pottery plates, glasses, and utensils.

As relaxed as porch dining may be, it must never look careless or hastily slapped together. The reason you and your guests go outside in beautiful weather is to enjoy Nature's summertime beauty. Do not spoil any of it with second-rate comforts.

House guests

One of the most pleasant ways to entertain guests is to get them outside—especially for

Even the tiniest of apartment balconies (the one shown both above and below is only 6 feet wide) makes a proper setting for entertaining out-of-doors. In addition to the dining table for four, a pair of hibachis has been set up. One cooks shrimps to be dipped in mustard sauce, the other cooks glazed pork tenderloin.

◄ A fenced-in deck, just a few steps away from the dining area adjacent to the kitchen, provides a marvelous setting for outdoor entertainment in beautiful weather. On not-so-perfect days, the party can be shifted in a flash from the deck through the French doors. The dining table enjoys a garden view, and it can be lighted with a hanging lamp.

meals. Dine them under a romantically lighted tree; give them luncheon on the terrace; produce an outdoor breakfast. For both you and your guests, these meals with scenery changes will make the visit more casual fun. Use your imagination and set a beautiful table.

How to serve outdoors

To entertain out-of-doors with maximum ease, you must be able to carry table settings and food as effortlessly as possible. A serving cart is one of the best answers to this problem. If your kitchen door is sufficiently wide, you can load your cart alongside your stove with

For an early morning breakfast for your weekend guests, served on a lakeside terrace, right, your table setting can borrow colors from the day itself. Pile fragrant limes and fresh green leaves in frosted yellow goblets around a bouquet of sunny daisies to make your centerpiece. At each place use a daisy-yellow juice glass and napkin. Just for fun, as place mats use big cloth daisies with yellow centers, visible through the serving plates.

A rooftop retreat, below, sheltered from sun, wind, and neighbors by a slatted wood screen, becomes a delightful outdoor dining room for a small luncheon party. A New Orleans-style wrought-iron grillwork fence and big redwood tubs of geraniums make a delightful frame for the surrounding countryside. Ivy trails from small pots fastened to the screen. The simple table setting, which contrasts with the intricate design of the iron tabletop, displays cool summer colors.

This charming shady setting for a seated outdoor meal features an unusual wraparound table that the home craftsman can build. The basis for the table is a simple trestle frame with a serving shelf at one end. Table legs consist of 2x4s, 30 inches in height. The table frame is made of two 2x6-inch horizontal strips, 10 feet in length, and three 21-inch-long 2x6-inch crosspieces. The legs are first bolted to the crosspieces, then the horizontal strips are attached, using lag bolts. The tabletop is made up of 1x6-inch boards, 40 inches in length.

To help convert a terrace into a room for parties and other festive occasions, a simple paneled bar, left, can be turned into a serving table for sit-down dinners. It can also be used as a buffet for help-yourself parties. Under the plastic-laminated top, several shelves provide ample storage space for barbecue gear and cooking utensils. When the bar is not in use for any serving purpose, it can be decorated with branches of leaves in a bowl. The brick wall behind the bar can also be decorated.

Shaded by an unusual triple-tiered umbrella, the simplest luncheon on a sundeck, above, turns into a romantic fete. Flowers and trailing ivy adorn the brick wall as well as the serving table, the latter a picnic table camouflaged with an embroidered cloth. Here, hot coffee waits alongside cups and plates.

dishes do not slip off the edges, and each should have handles to guarantee easy portability. A big wicker basket makes an additional handy receptacle for dishes, cups, napkins, and silver.

If informality is your out-of-doors entertainment style, use big paper napkins and provide wicker plates to go under your paper plates. Wicker plates underneath make it easier to cut food, and they also keep the paper plates from wilting. Plastic glasses are recommended for cold drinks. For hot drinks, it is best to have plastic holders equipped with handles for your paper cups. After your party is over, all the paper and plastic tableware can be removed directly from the table and discarded.

Equipment

The difference between just another cookout and truly elegant outdoor cuisine is often the equipment used. For barbecue buffs who make a hobby of suppertime productions on the patio, a built-in fire pit may be in order. On the other hand, if you plan your outdoor parties for many different locales, a portable grill is the best

Red geraniums growing in pots on the terrace below set the decorating scheme for the table laid out for six guests. Flowers form the the centerpiece and backdrop, and they even decorate the cloth.

everything you need for your party and then wheel the cart to the festive site. If you are having a buffet affair, the cart can do double duty as a buffet table.

It is convenient to have several electrical outlets near your outdoor entertainment area so that you can plug in your casserole, coffee maker, and hot tray. If you cannot have electrical outlets outdoors where you need them, use several trivets equipped with candles.

The next best way to get outdoors everything you need for entertaining is to use several large trays. Each tray should have a gallery so that solution. If your portable grill is designed for indoor as well as outdoor use—that is, if it does not smoke—it can be used for winter cookouts in the kitchen.

Several factors can make outdoor entertaining more pleasant: imaginative outdoor lighting, facilities for outdoor heating, adequate protection from wind and smoke, alternative plans in case of sudden weather changes, and, in particular, the elimination of insects.

Effective pre-party precautions against insects range from the expensive and semipermanent— electronic mosquito traps and foggers, devices that dispense a bug-killing mist with no ill effects on humans—to the simple and temporary—insecticide-impregnated strips of paper, yellow light bulbs, and aerosol sprays. It is also an excellent idea to drain or disinfest swampy areas or stagnant water near your picnic spot.

For additional ideas, see *Outdoor Lighting*, p. 2325; *Outdoor Living*, p. 2334; and *Party Ideas*, Vol. 14, p. 2499.

The perfect grill for an outdoor party in a corner of your garden can be made from a steel drum lid set on pipe legs filled with sand. Underneath is a bed of coals, and on the lid is a grilling grate. A ring of benches arranged against the garden wall puts your guests just a skewer away from the foods you prepare for them.

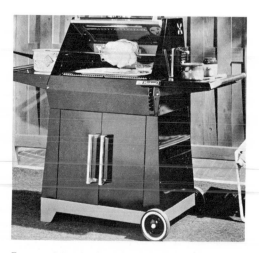

For precision barbecuing, a mobile wagon allows you to control temperature, fire pan level, and vents. It is equipped for every kind of outdoor cooking you will ever do— including spit grilling and smoking.

An apartment-sized outdoor grill, right, compacts into one small space a roasting spit, a lid that closes for smoking, and a handy little shelf on which to set basting sauces.

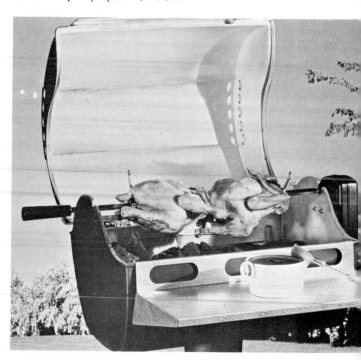

The home-built fire pit and serving table, above, are easy to make. Redwood-plank deck is held together by two redwood crosspieces. Cut a hole in center of the deck, insert asbestos flowerpot or other fire container that will hold the weight and heat of a charcoal blaze.

The patio fire pit, above, has been built into one of the terrace squares. Surrounding its brick walls, a floor of firebricks has been loosely laid over a bed of deep gravel that allows drainage and easy cleaning. This fire pit is ideal for grilling and for roasting marshmallows.

The charcoal starter, below, is a sure way to light charcoal quickly, without repeated applications of liquid lighter and kindling. Its tapered shape and patented draft ring get a fire going rapidly. Put a few sheets of crumpled newspaper in the bottom, add charcoal, and light paper. In 8 to 12 minutes, insert safety handle and lift off lighter.

The two-wheeled barbecue cart below provides a cooking area, counter space, and storage cabinets. The front work tray folds up when the cart is not in use, and its side wings fold over the grill or hibachi to form a cabinet. Paint it to match your kitchen; with proper ventilation, it may be used indoors. (For plans, order PP 3506-3.)

Proper Lighting Beautifies Your Home After Dark

Artificial outdoor lighting is needed for three reasons. First, and most essential, is the assurance of efficient and safe nighttime passage for family and guests going to and from the house. At the same time, trespassers are discouraged. Second, artificial lighting is provided for outdoor living areas so that the entire property—decks, terraces, and grounds—can be enjoyed without limit, whatever the hour. A third purpose, the beautification of the nocturnal surroundings, is a dual one. Making the evening garden pretty and inviting is part of it; bringing a lighted set of outdoor scenes through the windows is another. A view of softly lighted brick wall, floodlit fountain, and dramatically silhouetted trees, for example, is a welcome improvement over bleak black windows.

When you plan your safety lighting to prevent confusion and accidents, and to discourage

A hanging fixture placed on one side of a front door provides a symbolic gesture of welcome. The outsized lantern is in proper proportion to the large double door. A soffit light furnishes supplementary illumination.

Portable lamps vaguely reminiscent of Japanese lanterns impart a festive tone to special occasions. Spiked standards poke into the ground at casual angles; the lamps can also be fixed in permanent bases. Shades, in offbeat colors, are woven metal strips. Light shines softly through the weave to produce a colorful glow; stronger rays shine through top and bottom.

prowlers, look at your land as though you were a stranger to it. Study it from the publicly lighted boundary of the property to all entrance doors and to the garage. Consider toddlers and elderly people, and consider ice, slippery mud, and snow. Take careful note of all changes in level, even the slightest variations. Remember that walking on grass is one thing, but that an unseen change to rough stone can be hazardous. All steps and the tops of retaining walls should be marked.

All possible danger points must have adequate lighting without glare. Glare is a hazard in itself. And you must mark, with lighting, a route from the arrival point on your property to the front door. The house is the brightest single element and ideally the light should become dimmer and dimmer as it approaches the outer edges of the lot.

Lighting experts recommend for the main entrance door a pair of lights, one on each side,

Combination planter and garden light is equally appropriate as an entrance installation or as a patio accessory. The planter is built of terra-cotta-colored concrete blocks. The portable lantern has two metal cylinders—one black, one terra-cotta—mounted on an arched standard 41 inches high. Outdoor electrical outlet is needed for light cord.

Low fixtures with opaque tops provide a most satisfactory light for illuminating pathways: the shade prohibits bright light from glaring upward into pedestrians' eyes. The unobtrusive green-shaded mushroom fixture is a permanent installation. Its downlight dramatizes the verdancy of pachysandra ground cover.

66 inches above the sill. For side and rear doors, a single bracket placed on the keyhole side is sufficient. If the problem of trespassers is an important consideration, floodlighting that covers every inch of ground is the best idea; it provides lighting for safe walking as well.

When an outdoor area is lighted for nighttime living, some of the principles of indoor lighting are applicable. Three kinds of light are needed: a general diffuse illumination of the space, concentrated light for activities—the serving of food and drink, for example—and special lighting effects, such as the dramatization of a fountain or a piece of sculpture. Lighting consultants recommend a level of 3 to 5 watts per square foot; e.g., for 100 square feet of deck space, the total wattage should be 300 to 500.

Do-it-yourself outdoor lanterns hold Tiki lamps. Build a plain wooden box 6x6 inches and as high as needed. In the lid of the box, cut a circle with the same diameter as the lamp's brass bowl. Apply enamel finish. Tiki lamps, fueled with kerosene, are widely popular because they are portable and require no outside wiring.

Permanent moon-on-a-stick for deck or garden can be used alone or in a circular border. Spherical fixtures are available in clear or white glass or in plastic; they are made in many sizes. Globe is mounted on a threaded 1½-inch-diameter steel pipe which is screwed into a sleeve set in ground.

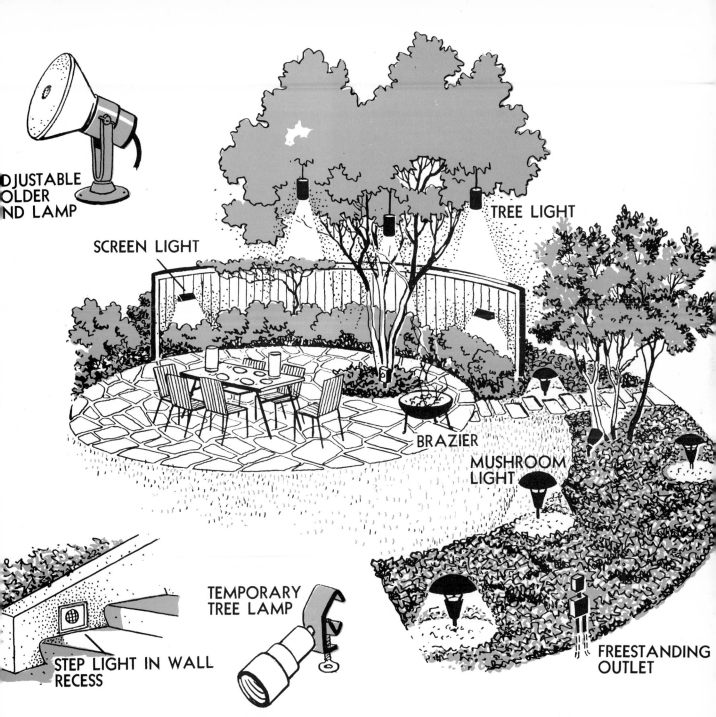

ADJUSTABLE HOLDER AND LAMP

SCREEN LIGHT

TREE LIGHT

BRAZIER

MUSHROOM LIGHT

STEP LIGHT IN WALL RECESS

TEMPORARY TREE LAMP

FREESTANDING OUTLET

The lighting of a garden utilizes as many varieties of fixtures as the interior of a house. As in a house, diversity itself is a charm, and each type of lighting has its own practical raison d'être. Conceiving this patio as a room, the "ceiling" has a chandelier—three canister lights hung from a tree to make a canopy over the dining area. The room's "wall" is a curved fence on which screen lights are fixed to cast a subtle glow both on the fence itself and on the plantings that follow its arc. Another outer boundary of the patio is also a curve—the bed of low flowers and shrubs. Here mushroom lights throw round pools of downlight to play up the color and texture of the flower bed as well as to light the stroller's path. Note the

junction boxes at the foot of the tree at right and near the mushroom cluster. These boxes, which provide outlets for plugs, consolidate wires which are then run into conduits underground to the electrical service center of the house. Planning and constructing this part of an outdoor lighting system is a job for a professional—electrical contractor, lighting consultant, or landscaping service. Two very useful additional fixtures are shown here: an adjustable holder and all-weather bulb that works as a floodlight (compare the installation in flower bed at right), and a clamp-on tree lamp. A more permanent fixture is the light recessed in the side of the outdoor stairway. The low-level bulb provides good light for tread and riser.

Lighting garden areas

Decorative garden lighting requires a different treatment from the utilitarian lighting of outdoor living spaces. Special dramatic effects are sought, once safety has been ensured by adequately lit pathways.

The garden is a space furnished with a wealth of interesting shapes—shrubs, trees, ponds, outbuildings, flower beds, stone walls—but these have no nocturnal existence until they are lighted. Floodlights can wash a whole area. Spotlights can shine from any level and can beam up or down or across space. Lanterns can hang from trees or perch on a post. Little lidded lights can dot a flower bed or encircle a well. There are as many attractive lighting techniques for outdoor space as for indoors. The object in lighting the grounds at night is to create a total effect, and the elements of lighting must establish an environment that is agreeable and interesting. While there can be, and should be, variety in brightness and in emphasis, nervous little bursts of light surrounded by blackness are to be avoided; so are black holes in a generally lighted area. Beckoning pools of light should entice strollers to explore plantings and architectural details in the garden.

In some large establishments, the gardens are secluded behind the house, and it is the facade of the building that its owners want to decorate with light. Floodlights, often used to illuminate landmarks, also have residential applications. Head-on floodlighting causes a flat effect unbecoming to most residential architecture. For dramatic modeling, floods should be placed at one side only; this placement is especially effective in lighting masonry structures with textural interest. A traditional house may

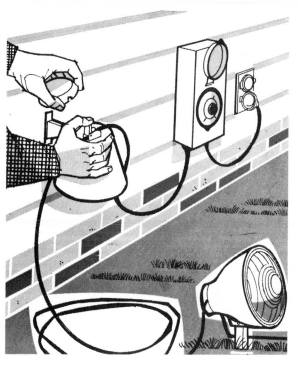

Portable 110-volt fixture, above, enables you to light whatever area needs it at any given time. A waterproof outlet powered by an extension cord run from the house can be staked anywhere in the garden. Tightly fitting spring covers protect the outlets when they are not in use. For safety's sake, use size-16 rubber-sheathed cord with sealed connections and molded and grounded plugs.

Twelve-volt system, above right, comes in a kit costing about $75. Such portable lighting equipment is more flexible and less costly than permanent installations. A kit contains up to six lights, 100 feet of cable, and transformer. You plug into an outdoor outlet and clamp the lights onto the self-sealing cable wherever you wish. Post lights, hanging lights, and walkway lights are available in similar kits.

A plant border, at far left, is lighted by three types of fixtures: a small light about 6 inches high defines the edges; a bright light about 2 feet high dramatizes tall plants and the texture of the pole fence; and a concealed flood picks out the foliage of a small tree. The lighting's first purpose here is calculatedly theatrical, but it also provides good general illumination for dining and entertaining.

Miniature lantern at entranceway strikes a note of hospitality. Its small scale and traditional form convey a pleasant suggestion of anachronism in a contemporarily styled planting of calladium and begonia. The installation provides adequate light, and incidentally demonstrates how to break a "rule" profitably. It is generally recommended that entry lights be mounted just above head height, but the unexpected ground-level location of this lantern gives an impression of strong individuality.

look its best if lights of unequal intensity flood it from two sides. Another popular device is the accent flood highlighting a fine doorway or other architectural detail.

Lighting with color

The color of the light you use is as important as its intensity. Foliage is embellished by blue-green or blue-white lighting, but is deadened by yellow bulbs. Cool colors add depth, and pale blues simulate moonlight. The fixtures should harmonize with the surroundings in shape, color, and style. They must be able to withstand weather and conform to all safety rules.

For the most modest kind of outdoor lighting on a small property, it is possible for a do-it-yourselfer to install the fixtures he needs if he has had experience in handling electrical installations and if he has good advice from his electrical or hardware dealer. If the project is more ambitious, or if the householder is inexperienced, one cannot too strongly recommend that experts be involved in the installation. Electricity is a force that must be respected. Any classified telephone directory will contain a list of electrical contractors who will install, repair, and maintain outdoor lighting.

The lighting of porches and patios, decks and terraces, is another matter that homeowners can work out with their electrical experts. If, on the other hand, an elaborately landscaped garden needs lighting designed expressly for it, another kind of expert enters the picture: the lighting consultant or the landscape architect. Both can be found in the classified pages, although in fewer numbers than contractors. Such professionals are artist-designers as well as experts in the engineering aspects of their fields, and no amateur can fill their roles.

Guide to lighting techniques

■ Silhouetting: establish it either by lighting the background and leaving a tree or sculpture dark against it, or by beaming light on the tree from a light source in the foreground.

■ Grazing: textures of masonry, tree bark, and hedges are best brought out by a light source parallel with the surface grazed.

■ Modeling: the third dimension comes to life if light is cast from at least two directions; the source should not be placed too close to the lighted object.

■ Highlighting: emphasis on a particular part of the landscape is accomplished by a down-light beam of appropriate strength.

■ Shadows: create them by imitating the sun, with one strong spotlight aimed at the tree or ornament whose shadow is wanted.

How do you supplement moonlight? The problem varies with the atmosphere you wish to create. Here, in a dusky meadow fragrant with azaleas, delicate Regency furniture, fine crystal, and china all suggest a mood of gracious elegance. The lighting chosen for this twilight supper is appropriately formal—a vermeil candelabrum holding tall white tapers. The more permanent lighting fixture is composed of three smoked glass bubbles on curved brass pads, supported by pencil-slim bronze stems. The globe fixtures are furnished with candlelight bulbs that simulate the flicker and shape of real candles. The effect is magical.

How to Make the Most
Of That Easy Outdoor Life

The merest hint of springtime is often enough to start people dreaming about living outdoors. Something about the fresh, fragile warmth makes you want to escape from winter clothes and winter rooms and revel in the welcome new atmosphere of spring. You can live gloriously with the great outdoors in one of two ways, depending on your outside space, the climate, and your life-style. The first is to move outdoors yourself; the second is to bring the outdoors into your home.

Moving out

When you have the open space and the climate is comfortable, the outdoors can become living room, dining room, playroom, even kitchen.

Your outdoor room can be as near as a patio just beyond the kitchen door—or as remote as a gazebo in the woods. It can be as elaborate as an air-conditioned garden room equipped with comfortable furniture, a stereo for music, a built-in refrigerator for drinks—or as simple as a hammock strung up between two trees.

You can do anything outdoors. Cook, dine, read, have a party, play games, lounge, bask in the sun, or, if there is a roof overhead, just watch and listen to the rain. Outdoor rooms can be wonderful for hobbyists: a poolside cabana might be an ingenious place to keep canvas and brushes for painting sessions on summer afternoons or model-making and tools for the latest father-son project. A garden gazebo, if it has shutters that lock up tight, could be the most delightful guest room in the world.

In the city, where personal pieces of the great outdoors are difficult to come by, rooftops can bloom into miniature sky-level gardens, where you can sit with a book or a friend. Minuscule ground-floor courtyards, perhaps rimmed with flowers, sprout lawn furniture and huge umbrellas. Even the tiniest city terraces can be transformed into decks for luxuriating in the fleeting sun.

Marvelous as the balmy outdoors can be, however, it holds its share of disadvantages that must be coped with and overcome—or sometimes surrendered to. At an outdoor barbecue, for instance, be sure to place the dining table upwind of the grill, for cooking odors and blowing smoke are not agreeable.

Use linen napkins, sturdy glasses, and inexpensive but solid pottery plates that will not fly away in the slightest gust, and provide deep ashtrays that will control their contents. Out-

Turn a garden into a living room by day, a splendid pavilion at night, with a deck of parqueted redwood propped a few inches above the ground, roofed with a flat ceiling whose beams form a star, and equipped with matching redwood lounge chairs with leaf-green mattresses. For privacy, a low fence of acrylic plastic shields the deck. To order plans for this pavilion, send for PP 3704-6.

door entertaining may be more casual than indoor, but making sure it is gracious can take just as much work. Always remember to be so well organized—and clearheaded—that you can cheerfully and efficiently capitulate to gale winds and move the party indoors.

Bringing the outdoors in

When no outdoor space is available for your personal use, or when the weather is unbearably hot and sticky, simply staying in the house, with windows shut against the humid heat and the air conditioning on, can be pleasant indeed.

Inside the house, the joys of summer can still filter through, even though you have screened

◄ Screened with vertical slats for privacy and light control, a backyard patio can become the setting for a party with all the poise of a well-appointed room indoors. Divided ceiling is fiber glass over simple stained beams. Half the floor is decked in redwood, for a dining- and game-table platform; half is covered with indoor-outdoor carpet.

out the noise and heat. You can furnish a cool living room with wicker, install trellis dividers, array potted leafy plants on the floor or hanging from walls and ceiling. Woolly winter rugs can be exchanged for cool linen and raffia ones. Beds can be dressed in gay, colorful sheets— and nothing more. A window can be curtained with miniature flowering plants on glass shelves. A hammock can be hung at a broad window, with all the books you have been dying to catch up on for months near at hand.

Choosing a room outdoors

No one who would like to create for himself a place in the sun (or shade) is limited to a conventional patio or terrace. Certainly a patio right beside the house or in the garden might be convenient for cookouts, but there are many imaginative ways to live outdoors.

In a warm climate, you might enjoy a lanai— actually an indoor room with its outside wall made of screening or louvered wooden doors that fold back to reveal an expansive view. A lanai can open onto the yard, a terrace, or a pool. Somewhat like the lanai is the combination indoor-outdoor room, a living or family room that extends into an area with a roof but no walls. Beyond this there might be an open patio or a garden. Such a two-part room is usually unified by continuous indoor-outdoor carpeting or by furniture of the same style in both parts. In bad or wintry weather, the outdoor section can be closed off with sliding glass doors, so the view can be admired all year.

For summer living more remote from the house, you might have a poolside cabana, with dressing rooms, bath, and dining area. Or you might prefer a more unusual garden room: a

Toadstool tables you can make in an hour: bases are red-clay drainage pipes sunk, flange end upward, into the ground and filled with sand. Tops, secured with latex concrete patching, are concrete steppingstones about 18 inches in diameter. These little do-it-yourself tables have endless possibilities: a row of them might hold cocktails for guests perched on the garden wall; a pair could be counter space for a buffet or, as here, for a barbecue chef's equipment; one alone could support a dining-table-sized plywood round for dinner parties; ring a tall toadstool with shorter-stemmed ones, as a permanent setting for games.

◄A terrace high above the city becomes a tiny garden when covered with grass-green outdoor carpeting and bordered with saucy geraniums. Ready for an iced-tea break, the terrace, shaded and partially shielded from crosswinds by neighbors' balconies above and at the sides, also is a cheerful spot for breakfast. With sliding glass doors opened wide, the large living room extends a few feet into the cool evening air, adding space for dancing, a cold hors-d'oeuvres buffet, or a portable bar. Lighting is provided during the day by the sun, at night by electric bulbs in cans sunk into pots beneath leafy plants at terrace ends.

lacy froth of ironwork just big enough for breakfast for two; a two-story stargazing platform; a lath house with a collection of orchids; an open party pavilion with walls of flowering vines and little twinkling lights.

Never underestimate your porch or breezeway for its summering advantages—it can be the most comfortable, attractive outdoor room of all. But if you do not have any outdoor structure and cannot build one, all you really need is a patch of grass. Just set up a few chairs, and relax.

Furnishing an outdoor room
So varied are outdoor rooms that furnishings for them are largely a matter of individual taste. Three requirements must be filled, however, to ensure long-lasting good looks and comfort from outdoor tables and chairs. They must be dur-

able and capable of withstanding sunlight, wind, and an occasional downpour when you have forgotten to take them in. They must be solidly built and well balanced, with wide-track legs, to prevent tipping in the wind. They must be constructed of practical materials that will not rust, mildew, or warp: aluminum, carefully painted iron, fiber glass, or rattan, for example, with coverings of nylon webbing, canvas, or sturdy vinyl. And cushions should be stuffed with mildew-resistant Dacron or plastic foam.

Even when you have bought the highest quality and most resistant-to-the-elements outdoor furniture, it must be carefully protected. Although a seat cushion is covered in vinyl, the needle pricks made by the stitching can let moisture seep in and cause mildew or odor.

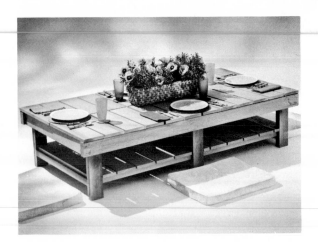

Turnabout table, top, has a hinged rear half that can be raised to convert table into bench, below—useful seating space at extra-big parties. When the back is folded down, the cushions are slipped onto the lower shelf and the unit becames a coffee table—or, with the cushions placed on the ground, a dining table for Japanese-style eating. To make this chaise-bench-table, order PP 3806-1.

Although it cannot boast a single blade of grass, this spacious outdoor living-and-dining area looks cool and serene. The ground is paved with loose-laid bricks over a 4-inch bed of sand. Walls are lattice fences, a lacy pattern that complements the white furniture. Instead of planted garden plots, flowers swing in baskets from the tree.

It is wise to have a large chest or closet handy, watertight and lockable, where you can stow your cushions and slipcovers during the weeks you will not be using the outdoor room, or in a period of bad weather, or whenever a storm is brewing. The seat of a built-in banquette in a porch dining area can open to hold the cushions. If you have an enclosed cabana or gazebo with indoor furniture, it is doubly important to keep all the shutters latched unless you are there.

For each kind of outdoor room, there are classic furniture types to consider: for porch or terrace, you might like the always fashionable rattan and wicker, with loose cushions covered in duck, vinyl, or even chintz. Redwood loungers with adjustable backs and thick, duck-covered

limitless fabrics, designs, and sizes. For good measure, load it with puffy pillows.

Floor coverings

When an outdoor room has a solid foundation, such as a plank deck or flagstone floor, an area rug can unite a furniture grouping and contribute a little softness underfoot.

You can select from a variety of rugs suitable for outdoor use; those made of woven or loopy linen or cotton can be machine washed. There are rugs of braided cotton and of Portuguese straw, which looks like heavy, large-scaled lace. The new synthetic leisure carpets are specially made for outdoor places; just for the fun of it, you might choose a synthetic carpet that looks for all the world like a freshly clipped lawn.

For privacy, plus the ambience of a leafy forest glade in this open space under a roof extension, a narrowly spaced trellis encourages flowering vines to grow luxuriantly.

Blooming like a huge blossom in a bower of greenery, the yellow umbrella with table attached makes a comfortable spot for alfresco meals on the bluestone terrace.

mattresses are just right for lounging, napping, and sunbathing. There are body-contoured fiber glass chaises. And metal frames webbed with strips of plastic that mold to the body.

For the garden, white-painted iron, cushioned for comfort, is classic. Or you might choose built-in stone sculptures for seats, mushrooms of concrete for dining tables, and concrete benches fitted with cushions to counteract their hardness. Redwood benches, curved around a fire pit or a tree trunk, could be an answer. For under the trees, you could have a pair of wicker swings, hung on chains from the branches, and tables with tripod legs that adjust to terrain gradations. Or the oldest classic of all and a perennial favorite, a hammock, in your choice of virtually

Build-it-yourself picnic table that is anything but run-of-the-mill can be put together with about $20 worth of redwood. For the top, frame narrow slats in alternating grain pattern with wider redwood boards (benches are made the same way). Be sure slats are closely spaced to prevent glasses from tipping. The three sections are supported and joined by end uprights. For instructions on how to build this table, order PP 3707-3.

Set on the side of a hill, the curving, cantilevered deck, shown below, is screened and shaded by a growth of young trees. On the deck are all the appurtenances that make outdoor living comfortable and carefree, including an open-pit barbecue and luxurious lounge furniture: a long bench, built along the curving lines of the deck, lazy wooden lounge chairs, and the traditional wooden picnic table—all constructed of beautiful and durable natural materials that seem particularly appropriate.

Walls and screens

Every outdoor room needs some measure of privacy, for part of the beauty and enjoyment of nature is being alone with it. Your shield against intruders can be sheltering trees, thick hedges, or acres of property stretching in all directions. But if nature has not provided you with screening, you can devise your own. Some of the man-made walls, partitions, and fences are interesting light filters as well as screens.

Wooden privacy-protectors can vary from the airiest lattice to the most solid, opaque boards cascading with potted geraniums. Walls of stone can be plain and unadorned to display the rugged beauty of the rock, or planted for prettiness in bloom. A brick wall can house an outdoor fireplace, then ramble on, perhaps festooned with ivy, to border the patio. You can build partitions of fiber glass, or rural rail fences covered with roses or honeysuckle, or even a barrier of half rounds of red-clay drainage pipe, stacked in overlapping fashion.

Ceilings

The only purpose of a ceiling on an outdoor room is to provide protection from the sun and the rain. If you have no intention of using the room in wet weather, the only roof you need is the spreading branches of a handsome tree. In a treeless garden, a ceiling of lattice or lath will pattern the shade and look especially attractive if there are walls or fences to match. Or you might pitch a canvas circus tent, gaily striped, with open sides and big gilt tassels.

If, on the other hand, it is your pleasure to sit outdoors and admire a summer rain, you need a solid roof. For an outdoor area room, such as a porch or terrace, that adjoins the house, the main roof can be extended into a broad overhang. Or you could peak the roof like a giant dormer and top your outdoor room with a marvelously high cathedral ceiling. For a detached, more remote room, you might build a cone-shaped roof like that of a medieval turret. Or, for a South Seas look, thatch it. If you want to keep dry but are reluctant to block out the sky view, you can make a roof of lacquered ceiling beams interspersed with sheets of fiber glass.

Decorating an outdoor room

Nature herself has provided more splendid scenery than any mortal could devise for a room

Even a front yard can be cordoned off into an outdoor room just as secluded as one behind the house. Here, a broad terrace, completely floored with brick, has large spaces between wood panels to preserve a clear view. Yet its brick parapet is high enough to guarantee privacy. At one end, a black iron grillwork gate opens on a brick path leading to garage and front walk.

outdoors. It is, in fact, the absence of contrived decoration and gimmickry that makes outdoor life refreshing and appealing. Think of the living tapestry of a garden, or ancient gnarled trees heavy with fruit, or the sea, lavender and blue and green, changing its colors to reflect the sky. Think of the charming pattern of butterflies by day and, at night, the miracle of lightning bugs, whose flickering light creates a spell mankind has never been able to duplicate.

Outdoor sounds and smells are as much a part of the decoration as are paintings and music indoors. There is a more subtle music in the meadow, in the voices of crickets and katydids, the songs of the birds, the peeping of tree frogs calling in the dark. The heady scent of jasmine and honeysuckle, the fragrance of banked white petunias, the pungence of geraniums, chrysanthemums, and phlox—all are very much a part of the outdoor decoration, and all are yours for the planting.

When you decorate an outdoor room, since you cannot hope to improve on Nature's fine hand, the wisest approach is to be sure your additions are harmonious with Hers. Provide yourself with comfort, but let Her inspire the color scheme of your surroundings.

For an outdoor place that is not a room at all but just a few chairs and loungers arranged with tables for refreshments under the sky, letting Nature be decorator is easiest of all; the very garden you and She have planned and grown may be all you need. Or shape a gazebo from clipped privet, with perhaps a central willow for its roof. Summer gardens have limitless possibilities for beauty and variety. The colors you choose depend entirely on your tastes, and on the atmosphere you wish to create. Set up your chairs and tables beside water, either still or running. Or set them in a nearby meadow where you perhaps have planted a few brambly roses to mingle with the wild asters and buttercups already growing there. And, of course, a tree is probably the most attractive spot.

Color

One has only to glance at a summer garden to realize that Nature loves every color under heaven. So your choice of colors that will mirror or complement Hers depends entirely on your taste and on the atmosphere you wish to create. A porch filled with old wicker, for example, painted white for unity but upholstered with a dozen designs in orange and white, can look as cool as a Popsicle against the background green of the trees. The naturalness of unadorned redwood or bamboo, with perhaps a leaf-patterned fabric, can make a rustic terrace seem like a wooded glade. Sometimes Nature likes to be surprised with paisley, or with one brilliant spot of solid turquoise in otherwise garden-print surroundings. Sometimes She might prefer neutral linen and leather-looking vinyl, so Her own brighter charms can take the limelight.

Color has its practical uses, too. A ceiling painted clear blue or green helps reduce glare much better than a white one (this is true not only for an outdoor room, but for one with many large windows). For the same reason, undersides of awnings and outdoor umbrellas are best limited to a cool, deep green or blue, no matter how riotous with stripes or flowers their sunward surfaces. By the sea, sun-absorbing ceiling colors like deep gray and green look coolest, and they make a wonderful foil for vivid patterns.

Light and how much to control it

During the day, except in dreary weather, all the light an outdoor room needs is supplied by the sun—occasionally too much, in fact, since one of the enemies of comfort is glare. With

The house is adapted from the timeless proportions of the French country style; the garden-patio shows a distinctly Japanese influence. There is no conflict, however; both the house and the patio are designed along lines of simple elegance. The pebble-floored, semicircular patio, divided from the dining room only by broad, sliding glass doors, doubles the summer entertaining area of the room.

Small and secluded, a deck adjoining the master bedroom can be a personal spa for private sunbathing, a convenient place for breakfasts for two. When there are guests, the deck, which also opens on a wide hallway, accommodates the party not far from indoor tables and becomes a literal doorstep to a living room as big as all outdoors. To make the deck a real part of the house's life style, its ceiling-high glass doors slide open, and the decorated translucent panel lets suffused light shine inside. On one deck wall is an enormous painting in weatherproof acrylics.

What a handy spot for a rained-out party. A permanent ▶ outdoor structure, such as this one, can greatly enlarge the scope of outdoor living and entertaining, whether it is erected beside a swimming pool, or built in a meadow or near a tennis court. The cabana shown here is of a simple and adaptable design, its conical roof covered with roughhewn cedar shakes and supported by sturdy cedar beams. Inside is a surprisingly large airy space with dressing rooms for swimmers, storage for swimming and entertaining equipment, and a shady conversation area.

glare, reading is an impossibility and admiring the view can cause a headache. Even chatting affords no pleasure when, facing the sun, you cannot readily see the features of your vis-à-vis. Work of any sort is highly difficult if the table surface is exposed to the sun.

The handiest, simplest way to eliminate blinding glare is with shades that unfold or unroll downward from ceiling or roof. Shades cut off light from the top and need be unrolled only part way. Decorative as canvas curtains may look tied back to pillars with chains or ropes, they are almost useless when it comes to this problem. Open, they let in every ray of sunlight. Closed, they envelop the room in darkness—and shut out the view besides.

Another way to control glare is with louvered shutters. The louvers are adjustable, so the shutters can be only partially closed, letting some light come through. For even more regulation, you might want to have a double bank of shutters—one above the other. With this arrangement, half the opening can admit full sunshine, the other be shielded against it.

Nighttime presents an altogether different problem, as anyone knows who has ever sat on a terrace as dusk deepened into darkness, talking to disembodied voices and the glowing ends of cigarettes. Outdoor lighting should not, of course, be bright. That creates unnerving contrasts. No matter what fixtures you choose, keep the wattage low.

When an outdoor and an indoor room are separated only by sliding glass doors or fold-back shutters, harmonious color schemes and furniture design can unite them into one gigantic space. The dining deck here borrows its fire from the upholstery colors of an otherwise neutral adjoining living room. Patterned tabletop and cushions repeat hues of redwood floor and natural-slat sun screens. Unpainted wicker furniture echoes the natural look of the living room. With the arrival of winter, the wicker is moved to an indoor family room, which also adjoins the living room. Other deck furniture: pull-up, canvas-slung chairs, benches topped with fat orange patterned cushions.

A ranch house conversation- and -▶ dining-terrace, set among acres of Kentucky pasture land, is carpeted by a man-made version of the famous bluegrass. The weatherproof imitation covers the entire area. Club chairs, of vinyl strips and cushions the color of the carpet, have painted-aluminum frames. For cocktails or coffee, a slatted-top ashwood-and-aluminum table. For dining, the table can be replaced with a folding card table supporting a plywood round and covered with a floor-length cloth trimmed in matching blue.

What to–How to–When to Plant Your Garden

First choice for all-summer color in the garden must be annual flowers. With little care they bloom continuously from early summer to fall, unlike any other kind of flower. Their range in color, size of bloom, and height of plant is so great that from annuals alone you can choose the ideal plant to fit any garden decorating need. For example, to create a strong color note, giant hybrid zinnias are an excellent choice. Their massive flowers often exceed 5 inches, the foliage is lush and green, and the color range from white through pastel to rich reds and yellows makes planning varied color schemes an exciting and rewarding experience.

Plantsmen have bred height regulators into the different types of zinnias. By checking heights given in seed catalogs or on the labels that come with trays of plants you buy at garden centers, it is possible to plan a whole border of zinnias alone so that tall varieties will be at the back and dwarf ones in front where they belong. When zinnias reach their mature height, they sprout side branches that prolong the flowering all summer.

From a decorator's viewpoint, planting zinnias in masses of one color is in better taste than using mixed colors. A dozen plants of coral-pink next to rose-pink zinnias or clear yellow beside rich orange are possible color combinations.

Flower favorites for outdoor planting

Several hundred different kinds of annual flowers are temptingly described and pictured in seed catalogs. Of all these, every gardener

Yellow Zenith zinnia, left, is typical of the cactus-flowered type. Bushy 2½-foot plants carry big 5-to-6-inch blooms on long stems, ideal for cutting to make dramatic indoor flower arrangements. All zinnias need full sun most of the day. Space young plants of these giant varieties at least 18 inches apart. Wide spacing keeps plants healthy.

Two more of the six separate colors of Zenith-type zinnias▶ are pictured at right: Torch, bright orange, to the rear, and Rosy Future in front. A sure way to get a pleasing and uniform effect in a flower border is to plant varieties of the same type of zinnia together, since all of them will have similar plant habit and style of bloom, as illustrated here.

has his favored few. We have selected a number that have special merit, not only for their color and decorative value in the home landscape but also for their suitability as cut flowers to enjoy in arrangements.

Garden books often suggest that one plant a collection of annual flowers in rows in a cutting garden. This would be a fine idea where space exists for such a luxury. Few home-owners, however, will have a plot of ground in an open sunny area that can be set aside exclusively for this purpose.

As a simple compromise, try planting annuals more lavishly around your home. Make flower borders deeper—up to 6 feet from front to back. Or select places where bold masses of annuals will add sparkle to an other-wise monotonous landscape.

By setting a dozen or two plants of one variety in a large clump, the plants widely spaced to give them room to grow, their land-scaping value is greatly enhanced. Moreover, you can cut enough flowers from each clump to make buxom bouquets for the house without robbing the garden and leaving it colorless.

Luxurious Gloriosa Daisies

Gloriosa Daisies are a striking example of these double-duty flowers. Nothing is more sensational in midsummer than a patch of two

Gloriosa daisies, bright show-offs of the garden world, are really rudbeckias. Their blossoms are five inches across, colored in a splendid combination of mahogany and gold. Plants grow to be three feet high and are attractive when grouped in clumps of six.

Vividly colored trumpets of spicy scent, vining nasturtiums climb this rough stone wall. Nasturtiums are annuals, grow best in infertile soil, bloom about sixty days after trans-planting. A variety of colors is available. Nasturtiums leaves are a tangy addition to salads.

dozen plants glowing under the summer sun. Each 2-to-3-foot plant, carrying a dozen or more flowers, is like a huge bouquet. Even when flowers are cut frequently, there are always enough left for landscape effect.

Gloriosa Daisies grow like weeds, from seed. Sow them in a little nursery bed, and transplant when they are a couple of inches high, spaced no less than 18 inches apart. Or seed can be scattered over freshly dug soil and raked in. When the seedlings are big enough, thin out surplus plants or transplant them elsewhere in the garden. Some plants from an early sowing will behave like annuals and will flower the first summer. The rest will not be large enough to bloom until next year. Gloriosa Daisies are really hardy perennials.

Other garden favorites

Nasturtiums are tender, cannot stand cold, and are hard to transplant. Therefore, when the weather is warm, sow the seeds where you want the plants to grow. Buy larger packets of seed, such as the ounce or 2-ounce sizes, to make an edging for a long flower border or path. Once they start to flower, you will never be without enough for indoor arrangements.

Ageratum comes slowly from seed and is not easy to start indoors. It is better to buy plants at the garden market. These plants will be in full bloom by early summer to brighten borders and paths with ribbons of color.

Varieties of petunias are grouped in seed catalogs under descriptive headings. The multiflora varieties grow about a foot high and their blossoms average 2 inches. As the name implies, they flower profusely and are best suited to mass planting where you want a bright swatch of color. Grandifloras have larger flowers. Some of them, such as the Cascade varieties, are especially suited to planting in window and planter boxes. Both single and double petunias lend themselves to lush arrangements. Petunias are especially spectacular when planted in hanging baskets.

Velvety, sweet-scented petunias come in exotic shades like magenta, purple, and pink, and in a variety of sizes. Dwarf petunias blend well with fuzzy blossoms of the ageratum (both are shown here). Both flowers grow slowly, so seedlings should be purchased from a greenhouse.

Verbena boasts luxurious spikes of white, pink, or red flowers. It grows best near warm areas, and is a good choice for hot spots like sidewalks or patios. Dwarf varieties of verbena have been developed that grow quickly and spread until the soil becomes matted.

The abundant luxury of the rose

Roses have everything going for them—exotic fragrance, endless variety of colors blended together in ever-changing patterns and hues, satiny-textured petals, and buds and blossoms carved in sculptured perfection of form. It is fascinating to watch a bloom unfold from the time the first petal slips out of the green calyx until it becomes full-blown, beautiful to behold. No wonder more rosebushes are planted each year than any other kind of shrub.

Roses are indeed hardy shrubs, comprising a more varied family than most people realize. In bush size, they range from 6-inch miniatures to 10-foot hardy species and shrub roses.

Hybrid teas are the obvious first choice of all roses. Most everyone knows that they grow best in deeply prepared beds, alone, or edged with low flowers that will not interfere with the care of the rose bushes.

Floribunda

In recent times floribunda roses have gained great popularity because by nature they produce more flowers throughout the year. They are rugged, mix well with other low garden flowers, and are excellent as low hedges or edgings of walks, as supplementary color for new evergreen and shrub landscape plantings, and as accent and background plants in flower borders. While their blossoms are borne mostly in clusters, many come on individual stems, ideal to cut for arrangements.

Grandifloras

Roses classed as grandifloras grow taller than floribundas. Otherwise, they are used like them

The hybrid tea rose Valencia is highly prized for the rich orange-apricot color of its perfectly formed buds and blossoms. Such choice flowers deserve a place in every landscape where their beauty can be admired at close range, much as they are pictured above. Their copper petal tones blend beautifully with those of the clematis.

◄ Floribunda roses, such as shell-pink Gay Princess, left, are not only a reliable source of exquisite blossoms for cutting from late spring through fall, but also fill many landscape uses. This rose bed frames the patio. It is edged with purple violas for color contrast and to furnish flowers in spring before the roses bloom. Low annual flowers, such as sweet alyssum, are good edgers too.

in landscape plantings. Queen Elizabeth is everyone's first choice in this class. It blooms repeatedly all summer: great, fragrant, rose-pink flowers swaying on long thornless stems, superb for cutting, eloquent in arrangements.

Climbers

Free use of climbing roses transforms the landscape into a showplace at the smallest expense for plants and the least amount of maintenance. Climbers trained over walls or fences, on lattice or arches, or as cover on posts improve landscape design by relieving the flatness of lawn.

The cast stone figure of Kuan Yin, goddess of mercy, rests serenely in this tranquil setting. Simplicity of design is the keynote here. The clean lines of thin-stemmed shrubs are repeated in their shadows, cast upon the bamboo screen. The rounded stones exemplify the Oriental mood of this enclosed garden nook. Pebble mulch knits the elements together.

Day lilies and daffodils—a natural pair

Some flowers naturally belong together in the garden. Two that are just right for each other, pictured on these pages, are day lilies, or hemerocallis, and daffodils.

The reason for this becomes obvious when we consider how these two plants grow. Daffodils are the first showy flower of spring. Even in northern gardens, by April their blooms fill flower borders with golden color.

It does daffodil plants no harm to pick blossoms with long stems provided their leaves are left. Arrange daffodils with such flowers as forsythia and pansies for a touch of spring in the house.

After daffodils finish flowering, the inviolate rule is to allow their leaves to mature and die down naturally. During this process, bulbs gather strength to flower again next year. This is the daffodil's brief period of ugliness.

Delicate day lilies

Day lilies are late starters, not blooming until summer. When daffodils are in flower, day lily leaves are only tufts of green. Soon, however, the leaves, which closely resemble those of daffodils in color and shape, stretch, arch over, and cover the ground. Therefore, by interplanting clusters of daffodils between clumps of day lilies, the unsightly yellowing daffodil leaves are hidden from view, and both flowers thrive. This is called companionate planting.

Daffodils are the most permanent of all bulbs—true perennials. By checking bulb catalogs, you will discover that varieties are grouped according to character or design of flower. There are eleven basic divisions. Three are pictured to the right: small-cupped Verger at upper right; large-cupped Duke of Windsor at upper left; and triandrus hybrid Liberty Bells bottom left. Daffodils are fragrant.

◄ The day lilies pictured to the left are only a small sampling of the thousands of varieties that will thrive with a minimum of care in the average garden. Many local nurseries now stock a good selection, grown in containers. These plants can be set out while in bloom without setback. Since their flowering time varies, you can mix colors in the border for any period from June until September.

Day lilies are first choice for almost every landscape situation: sun or part shade; wet or dry soil; flower borders or rough banks; fillers in front of shrubs or evergreens. This tough, hardy perennial ranges in height from under 2 feet to 6. Every tone of yellow, orange, pink, rose, to deep red and purple is found among the thousands of varieties now available.

Cut blossoms are bold dramatic material for arrangements. In using them, however, be aware that each flower lasts only for a day. Moreover, most varieties do in fact open only in daylight as their name implies, and close by nightfall unless ready-to-open buds are held in the refrigerator. Most people prefer to cut individual blossoms or short stems rather than the whole stalk that invariably holds many buds that would bloom in the garden over a period of two or more weeks.

Spring landscapes

Creating effective landscape plantings with spring bulbs is not nearly as difficult as working with other garden flowers. New bulbs, planted in the fall, are almost sure to bloom satisfactorily provided they are planted according to instructions in good soil, dug deeply, and enriched with bulb food. Each bulb has embryo buds and leaves stored inside, ready to respond and to grow.

Quality bulbs are graded according to size. Only flowering-size bulbs are exported by the Dutch growers. Thus, a dozen daffodils or tulips of one variety, planted in a group, will all bloom together on stems of uniform height. This makes it easy to plan color combinations in flower borders or beds. By giving some thought to their season of bloom, heights, and colors, it is possible to plan a continuous show.

Planting hardy bulbs

Hardy bulbs are planted in the fall, with few exceptions. It is true that some nurseries and garden centers plant small stocks of daffodils and tulips in pots that they store over winter and bring into bloom at their normal flowering time. They are convenient to plant, pot and all, for immediate color. You can use them in a pinch to brighten your grounds when you are entertaining friends or the garden club. Otherwise, plant them in prominent places that were overlooked in the fall.

Lilies are true aristocrats. No other flower from bulbs has such character. A cluster of

three stalks, each 5 feet high, topped with a dozen 6-inch-deep trumpets, has tremendous landscape impact. These tall lilies are of many colors—pure white, yellow, rose-pink, white marked with burgundy, even chartreuse. Lilies are best planted in the fall. For spring planting, select bulbs which have plump live roots.

Bulbs that bear one flower or flower cluster to a plant are ideally suited to mass in a precise pattern or formal bed. Dutch hyacinths and most tulips are the best examples. To get the effect of an even, unbroken color patch, set the bulbs not more than 6 to 8 inches apart.

Where and when to plant

You can get enough help from bulb catalogs or booklets that local bulb dealers will supply to plan a continuous succession of bloom in your garden. There are bulbs for all situations. Crocuses, scillas, snowdrops, hardy anemones, grape hyacinths, even daffodils grow surprisingly well in difficult locations where more sophisticated garden flowers would fail, such as under deciduous trees and shrubs, along a wild garden path, or in pockets of soil in rocky places. All bloom early in spring.

Though cut flowers of small bulbs like crocuses are difficult to arrange in containers, an entire clump, dug with a trowel and pressed into a shallow bowl, makes an interesting conversation piece. When the flowers fade, plant the clump back in the garden. When cutting tulips, let the two bottom leaves remain on the plant to conserve the strength of the bulb.

◀Dwarf spring-flowering bulbs have the proper height in a rock-garden setting. They are early flowering, too, a full month ahead of tall May-flowering kinds. The two tulips pictured far left are classed as Waterlily Hybrids or Kaufmanniana tulips. Centers of open blooms have contrasting colors as in variety Fritz Kreisler, top of picture. Pale blue Puschkinias complement yellow Fair Lady tulips, below, a fine example of effectiveness of mass bulb planting.

◀Tulips and onions might seem to be strange bedfellows but, as pictured at left, the gold and purple of this pair make a pleasant combination. Onions are classed as alliums in catalogs and garden stores. There are at least two dozen kinds grown in gardens, their heights ranging from one to 4 feet. Though the foliage of alliums smells like onions when crushed, the flowers of some kinds are sweet-scented. Alliums are hardy, their bulbs being planted in the fall. The taller kinds are exceptionally fine to cut for flower arrangements.

Crocuses are the beloved harbingers of spring in gardens, defying snow and frost. With amazing energy, white spears press up through grass and dried leaves, bursting into bouquets of brightly colored yellow, purple, blue, white, and striped cups. There are two general groups of crocuses: the winter-flowering species and the larger Dutch hybrids. The species bloom first. Orange-yellow Aureus, the Chrysanthus varieties, and lavender Tomasinianus may flower by late February even in the north when planted in a warm southern exposure against a wall. Crocuses cost less than other hardly bulbs, so plant them in broad patches where their color is most effective, as in front of and between evergreens and shrubs, and in rock gardens.

The opulent and hardy peony

Peonies have a record of a longer life span in gardens than almost any other perennial flower. Old clumps around country homesteads have outlived the first generation of occupants. The plants are remarkably hardy, surviving the winter of Canada and U.S. prairie states. Unfortunately, they languish in mild climates of the South.

Peonies, and a few other perennials such as Oriental poppies, should seldom be transplanted once they become established in the garden. Shifting plants is sometimes done when they are too crowded after many years; divide them and transplant with care. Failure to flower usually is due to a few common errors in choosing the place for the plants in the beginning. Peonies need full sun; deep soil; no crowding from other plants, particularly trees and shrubs; and shallow planting—the top of the crown of roots not more than 2 inches below soil level. After their first year, heavy feeding with a flower-garden fertilizer, a trowelful per plant, cut into the soil right after flowering time, is recommended. In fact, feeding often brings nonflowering plants back.

Peonies make big clumps and need plenty of space in borders. Fall planting is best, though young clumps sold in big baskets in bud or bloom will transplant well if dug with a big root system. Peony blooms are prime material for massive bouquets. Cut them as the buds crack and let them open indoors.

Growing the elegant begonia

Tuberous-rooted begonias are a challenge to the skill of the gardener, but a joy to behold

Peonies make massive clumps in the garden. Usually several buds are borne on each stem. Although larger blooms result from nipping off side buds, leaving only one to a stem, the floral effect is better when all buds are left to open one after another. Single and Japanese-type peonies, shown left, that have open centers, are preferred for landscape planting.

when grown successfully. Giant blooms with waxen petals are classed according to their resemblance to other flower forms, including camellia, rose, and carnation. Some have frilled or ruffled petals; others are edged with a deeper color, such as red on a yellow base. All the colors are exciting—pink, salmon, rose, yellow, crimson, or pure white.

A group of these begonias, growing in a shady spot, can be a source of pleasure all summer long, first for the beauty of their flowers poised above rich glossy leaves, and further for their unmatched elegance when floated in shallow containers or otherwise arranged to capitalize on each bloom.

Grow the large double kinds if your interest is first in perfect blooms. Multiflora varieties are well-formed, too. Though smaller, there are more of them; they are preferred for display in borders. Both types do well in window boxes or large planters. Hanging begonias have trailing stems, ideal to plant in hanging baskets and window boxes.

Begonias grow best where they get light shade all day, never full sun. Keep them watered and fed with a weak solution of liquid fertilizer during the hot, dry days of summer. Use less water when they stop blooming, and, when the leaves fall, stop watering entirely, cut off the dead stems, shake the soil from the tubers, and store them at a moderate temperature in boxes filled with dry peat moss. In spring, start the tubers in flats filled with peat moss or leaf mold. After they sprout, move plants to harden in a cold frame. About two weeks after it is safe to plant tomatoes, begonias can be moved to the garden.

Soil for tuberous begonias should be lightened with peat moss, leaf mold, compost, or even sand where soil is clayey since the plants need good drainage. Humus holds moisture and plant food where the roots can get it. The same soil is used for hanging begonias like the ones growing in attractive containers on the fence. Plants in baskets need frequent watering in sunny weather.

Choosing the appropriate ground cover

Several dozen plants qualify as desirable and valuable ground covers. Your choice of any of these will be determined by the situation in which the plant is to be used. The most universal use of a ground cover is as a substitute for grass. It can be grown successfully where a lawn is impossible, as in the dense shade under trees; on steep banks which are difficult to mow; or as a change of pace to add texture and variety to the landscape.

Several good illustrations of ways to employ ground covers to advantage are shown on these pages. Note that one type of plant spreads over the ground by trailing stems or underground runners. These plants should be used only where they can be controlled easily by clipping with shears or cut back with a rotary mower, or their underground growth contained by adjoining paving or walls.

To put these plants where they can spread into flower beds would be a mistake. However, there are now good metal or plastic edging strips that, when sunk into the ground 4 to 6 inches deep, are excellent barriers that

An entrance garden, separated from the driveway only by a low planted strip, conserves space without sacrificing the elements of contemporary design. It does not take much in the way of plants or upkeep either. Each circular bed is only 50 inches in diameter and holds a dwarf juniper and petunias. Metal edging retains soil.

Strawberries, used extensively as a ground cover in the West, make an interesting "lawn." The favorite is Fragaria chiloensis, a wild species native to the Pacific Coast states, pictured lower left. It has small white flowers followed by brightly colored fruits. Plants grow 6 to 8 inches tall but height can be kept low by mowing. This planting successfully unifies landscape elements.

Naturally compact junipers and a crushed stone mulch combine for a neat semicircular design in the landscape plan. This bed, below, is easy to maintain as well as being attractive. The gentle curves that mark the lawn's edges are easier to mow than sharp corners. All trees, shrubs, and perennials in this plan are kept within definite beds; continuous mowing patterns are unbroken. The stone mulch is 1 to 2 inches deep, which is enough to keep down weeds. Metal curbing keeps stones off grass.

Perennial ajuga or bugle makes a solid carpet under the old spreading pear tree in the garden pictured to the left, and also is a capping for the stone retaining wall. Ajuga is a rugged ground cover for lightly shaded places, spreading quickly to make a green mat that is covered in spring with blue flowers. There is a lovely bronze-leafed variety too. It is wise not to plant ajuga near flower beds.

Two small-leafed ground covers have been utilized in the center picture, below, to cover the bank neatly and to keep soil from washing down onto the terrace. Around the lead figure, fountain bird bath, and beyond, evergreen vinca, also called periwinkle or myrtle, extends up to the daffodils. In spring, vinca is sprinkled with blue flowers. Bowles Variety bears bigger, brighter flowers.

Hardy liriope or lily-turf circles this restful expanse of lawn in a Texas landscape, bottom of page. Liriope is hardy up to New York City, though it is used more extensively in the south as an edging and ground-cover plant. It is equally satisfactory in shade or sun. The plants spread rapidly by underground runners. In summer, spikes of their blue flowers stretch above the foliage.

prevent roots from penetrating the soil beyond the planted area. These curbs also keep soil from washing onto paved walks and patios.

Growth patterns of ground covers

Some ground covers have one stem or trunk. Their pattern of growth is low and only the branches are spreading. Creeping junipers and cotoneasters are good examples. When they are first planted, with proper space between the plants, the bare ground between them can be covered with mulch such as bark chips, chunk peat moss, pebbles, or stone chips. Organic material will in time mix with the soil and add humus. In the case of stone chips and pebbles, it is sometimes advisable to lay down a plastic sheet over the ground before spreading the stone mulch. This will prevent the soil from working up from below.

Mature size of ground-cover plants will determine how far apart they should be set. Pachysandra might be spaced 8 to 10 inches apart, whereas creeping junipers could be 2 feet apart. Naturally, closer planting gives quicker results but at added cost.

Gardening in planters

Special care is needed in designing plant arrangements in containers and planter boxes because a complete landscape must be compressed into a tiny space. Every plant used should carry its weight. No short-lived material or varieties which are quickly in and out of bloom have a place in planters. In outdoor living areas, summer color should be a first objective since this is the time of year when a patio is most used. Annuals and bedding

Annuals take naturally to pot or planter culture, so they are ideal to decorate a patio or deck where garden space is limited or nonexistent. You can choose many forms of hanging baskets for annuals, but this ceramic container, above, is less subject to drying out in the wind. An inch-deep layer of gravel in the bottom, covered with a sheet of ½-inch fiber-glass insulation, provides drainage.

Aluminum-mesh pot covers, pictured left above, take only 20 minutes to put together. Glamorize your potted plants quickly and inexpensively by setting them in these decorative cylinders. To assemble, first make a pattern of heavy paper to fit the size of pots used. Add ½ inch to circumference length so the metal will overlap for fastening. Cut mesh, available at lumber yards, with tin snips. To tie ends together, overlap ½ inch and crimp metal tips of cut edges through holes of adjoining mesh. When finished, paint black and slip over pots when dry.

Planters like the one to the left are mini-gardens designed to bring color right into the outdoor living area. White petunias and red geraniums, set against a dark evergreen and nestled beneath a small shrub, provide all-summer enjoyment and surplus flowers for cutting. This planter was built as an extension of the deck and bench. The wood should be treated with a wood preservative.

plants suited to the exposure, whether it is full sun or shade, are prime subjects.

In larger planters, designed for year-round landscape effect, both flowering and woody plants have their value. However, all evergreens and shrubs must be dwarf varieties that will not get out of scale after a year or two. Plants having interesting forms are also preferred. Their shape may be natural or controlled by pruning.

More maintenance must be given container plants. After all, they are always seen at close range. Snip off dead flowers before they fall, prune away dangling branches, and stake floppy plants. Keep a sharp lookout for insect pests; aphids multiply with amazing speed on tender new shoots. A couple of applications of a flower-garden spray, put on ten days apart, should take care of them.

Yellow Nugget marigold is naturally dwarf and will not get too large for the planters, above, even by late summer. Its clear yellow, fully double, 2-inch blooms are long lasting, supplying continuous color until frost. Snipping off dead flowers keeps the plants neat and encourages more bloom. There is enough soil in these planters to keep the plants going with an occasional light feeding.

A glazed-brick planter can be yours in 30 minutes. Just stack loose bricks, as pictured below, on the patio in any shape, size, or location your fancy dictates. Scale the planter to accommodate the number and size of plants on hand. Choose a site that is best for your plants. Foliage plants from indoor windows need shade and protection from heavy rains. Set potted plants in moist peat.

This step-up planter, below, filled with spreading evergreens, demonstrates how to change a problem slope into an easy-care area. Each planter is mulched with shredded bark and faced with river stones. The only maintenance needed here is feeding and watering. Dwarf evergreens suited to this type of planter include junipers—dwarf Pfitzer, Golden Prostrate, Hetzi Blue Pfitzer.

When the garage or the paneled wall of the house faces your outdoor living area, add a narrow planter bed as part of the permanent furnishings. A foot of garden loam, kept in place with a brick or redwood curbing, is enough to use. Supplement hardy evergreens with geraniums, petunias, and coleus, for season-long color, or cover the wall with espaliered shrubs.

In the semicircular raised planter bed below, Spanish Brocade marigolds and Irish Eyes Gloriosa Daisies make compatible planter mates. Their colors blend well and pick up the tones of both the planter and the paving. Spanish Brocade, a greatly improved French marigold, has extra-large yellow blooms accented with red.

Designing mini-gardens

Limitations of space need not prevent you from trying your skill in adding touches of color to outdoor living areas with little pockets of flowering plants. The capsule-size garden often has greater charm than more extensive plantings. Concentrated effort can bring big rewards, brightening dull areas of your yard.

Careful planning in the beginning has many advantages, with emphasis on the plants themselves. Each plant and flower ought to be chosen for a specific reason, such as its color as part of an overall color scheme in which floral tints, pavings, even the color of patio furnishings harmonize. Plants with staying power, either as flowering subjects or as green background, help to minimize the maintenance problem and eliminate the necessity of re-

placing spent plants with fresh material. Then there is more excitement in growing something new, like All-America Selections annuals, thus giving yourself the satisfaction of judging their qualities. You will find them featured in nurseries and garden centers.

Planter beds built into or on the ground are easier to manage than individual containers. For one thing, they do not dry out quickly. There need be little concern, too, about bottom drainage, unless the bed is surrounded by a solid wall. Even then, you can leave openings in the base of the wall through which excess water can leak out. If soil is poor, give it body by mixing in peat moss or humus. Add slow-acting fertilizer, such as one having an organic base, mixing it deeply into the soil. Give the plants liquid fertilizer during the summer.

You can add instant color to your terrace, steps, or patio with brick-collared nursery flats filled with blooming annuals, such as petunias, dwarf marigolds, and impatiens. Local nurseries and garden centers sell 16x20-inch flats or trays of bedding plants in bloom. Place the flats in strategic spots needing color and conceal their wooden sides with dark gray bricks.

These stepping-stones, right, are made of brick, set in sand, and held with a frame of 2x2-inch redwood headers. To keep the brick from shifting, use a basket-weave pattern and miter and nail the redwood headers at the corners. Fill space around the stepping-stones with ground-cover plants. English ivy is at left and ajuga to the right. Small-leafed ivies are neater in their growth and need less pruning.

In this terrace planting, below, more space is available so both perennials and annuals have been used. Tall perennials including phlox, day lilies, and Gloriosa Daisies serve as a background for masses of petunias in front. All these flowers are growing in ground beds. Here early spring-flowering bulbs such as tulips and daffodils, even pansies, would make a pretty picture viewed through the terrace doors in spring.

Planning an efficient tool shed

The tool shed or garden work center will pay its way many times over on almost every suburban property. It takes a surprising amount of equipment just to keep the lawn mown, fed, watered, and treated for pests and weeds, not to mention pruning hedges, shrubs, and evergreens, carting leaves and rubbish around, and potting the house plants. Then there is the problem of storing the patio furniture, bird bath, and barbecue grill over winter. Too often all this stuff lands in the garage, making it a disaster area.

The only way out is to get a separate tool shed. Depending upon space available, it can be either a separate structure, or attached to the house or garage, or backed onto a fence, as pictured on these pages.

Before deciding on the size of the shed, survey the amount of equipment it must hold —and multiply by two. Dead storage is one thing, but during the active garden season you will need elbowroom to get equipment in and out. After all, the major objective in having such a building is to organize equipment and supplies and simplify your work.

Locate the shed where it is convenient to unload supplies from the car and, if possible, also near the garden. As for design, this depends upon its total use. Buildings used solely for storage may be like a series of large cabinets with doors. Floors flush with ground level or garden walks are best where wheeled equipment is being stored.

Larger structures can be designed as garden hobby workshops. A roof overhead is important because you can then work inside, rain or shine. Weatherproof siding adds further to your comfort and improves conditions for storing supplies affected by moisture. It is wise to have a door that can be locked to keep children from getting into supplies. When the garden room must double as a rainy-day playroom, build eye-level cabinets with doors that can be locked to store garden chemicals and fragile equipment.

The workshop designed for pursuing the hobby of gardening seriously will have additional refinements such as work space for potting seedlings, making cuttings, growing plants under artificial lights; space for storing roots and bulbs; bins of soil-mix ingredients; wall charts for timing garden operations; and shelves of books, catalogs, and plant-society bulletins. Maybe there could even be space for a comfortable chair in which to settle down and read garden lore, undisturbed by TV or the telephone.

You can make your storage shed a part of the garden fence or privacy screen. This one fits neatly into the landscape and is handy to the garden. The unit is 14 feet long and 44 inches deep and is sided with 1x4-inch resawn western red cedar. The floor of the shed is level with the walk for ease of rolling equipment in and out. Both are of concrete, and were poured together. The roof overhang prevents rainwater from running into the building. The interior walls and doors are in contrasting colors to relieve the neutral gray of the building. Shelves and wall hooks double this shed's storage capacity.

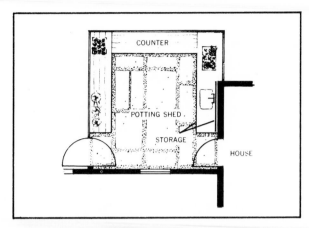

Gardening tools and a wide assortment of potting equipment are kept at hand in this weather-resistant aluminum potting shed. The plan, left, shows how you could build it at the rear of almost any house—and it can do double duty as a childproof mud room or screened outdoor living area. There is a cold-water sink and convenient storage for pots and fertilizers in the redwood cabinet. Waist-high counter and plank shelves keep work at just the right height. A floor of river gravel and precast concrete stepping-stones is easy to keep clean and dry. The lath-and-screen sides let in breezes and sunlight. Aluminum is lightweight and easy to cut, so you could do all the structural work yourself if you wish, or hire a company that fabricates aluminum patio covers to put up the basic framing and provide the screening. The filtered sunlight coming through the sides and roof is enough to keep house plants in prime condition all summer long.

Easy-to-Build Projects for Your Child's Play Space

There are certainly plenty of practical, logical reasons why your children should have imaginatively designed play areas. Climbing strengthens leg muscles; vigorous outdoor excercise builds healthy bodies; if children are busy on their own, mother can concentrate on housework free of distractions. But for the parent who watches his child enjoying facilities like these, the shining eyes and happy smile are enough to make work worthwhile, without the practical rewards.

When you plan a play area for your children, make sure to leave something to their imaginations. You remember how much enjoyment you found in a vacant lot when you were young, stimulated only by the prodding of curiosity. Your children have the same reactions, although they also enjoy the various materials for play—things to push and move, sit on, or ride in; structures that need only be named to assume an identity: to become a fort, a ship, a horse, a train. Sandboxes are infinitely appealing and play-stimulating; so are swings, whether the manufactured variety or used tires hung on ropes. For small areas, consider steps: a double stairway does not take much space and provides climbing exercise aplenty.

Safety precautions

Keep safety in mind as you prepare the play area. Fences provide protection from traffic,

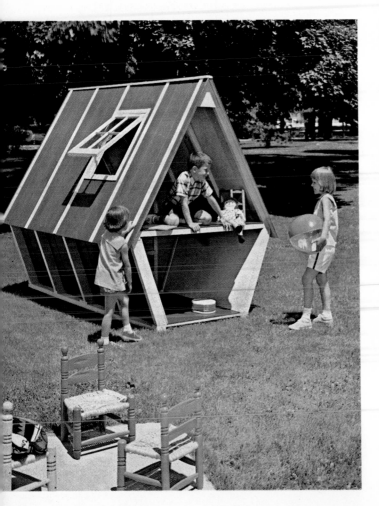

The perky but simple pentagonal playhouse shown at left, executed by a do-it-yourselfer, required very little in the way of materials: 2x4s, to support the inclined lower wall; 2x2s, for the peaked roof; plywood, for floors and walls; and stock millwork, for the skylight. The plan offers a floor-through room at the first story and a balcony, reached by a tiny two-rung ladder, on the second.

Magic of a tree house is irresistible. This one, shaped like ► a ship, can be built even where there are no trees, and, because "cabin" has both window and door screening, can be used for overnight voyages. Sturdy dowels form ship's ladder. Solid posts, cross-bracing, and stout railing are all safety features worth noting. While this house is ship-shaped, it is not loaded with nautical details; they might cramp children's imaginations. Some days, they may think it looks like a train or a houseboat. Possibilities are limitless; with a rope, children can lower a basket for you to load with a picnic lunch. Send for PP 3704-4.

and can be decorative as well as useful. Locate the play area, if possible, where mother can conveniently supervise the activities from time to time. A location in view of the kitchen and first-floor bathroom is ideal. Another point to keep in mind: the back door entryway should have hooks and cabinets for play equipment at child level to encourage neatness.

When you plan play structures for your children, be sure to include boxes, cabinets, and/or bins to hold the equipment they will use in active play.

For instance, if you build a small playhouse, why not add a "carport" that will protect wagons, tricycles, and doll carriages from the weather? Sandbox seats can be hinged to lift up; inside the boxlike enclosure under the seat will be tucked the pails, shovels, molds, and little cars that make sandbox play so much fun. A "cage" made from a wire trash basket will hold balls and toys.

Make provisions for the spills and messes that are part of childhood. If the play area has an easily hosed-off surface, the children can indulge in less-inhibited antics without fear of scolding. You may even join in, knowing that cleaning-up time will be minimal.

If you decide on concrete for a paved tricycle-riding area, paint in game circles and squares, or hopscotch markings, or a ticktacktoe diagram. With bright outdoor paint, these will look like abstract designs.

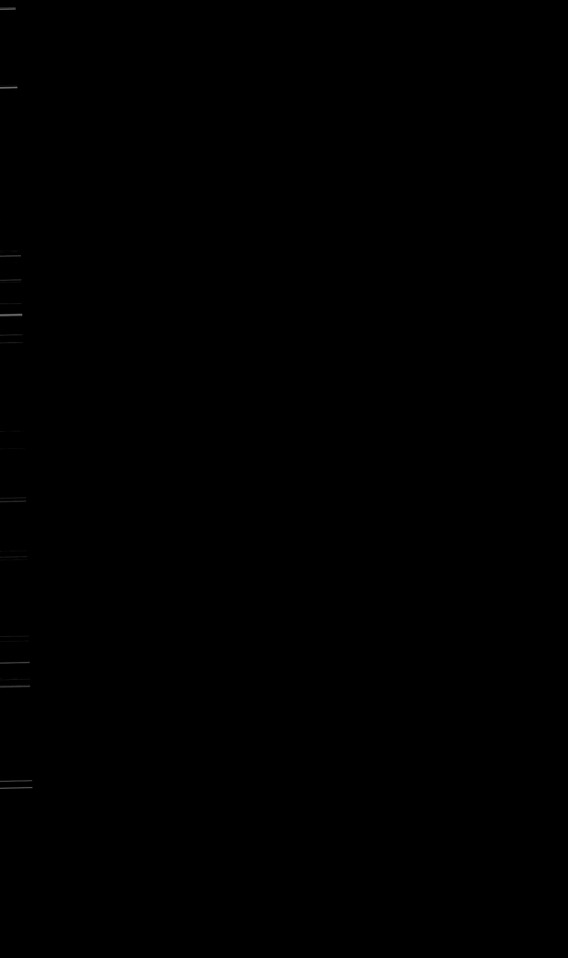

Two-level unit, above right, combines canvas and ¾-inch plywood. 2x4s make frame, plywood the box structures. Canvas is stretched and fastened over two lengths of spring-mounted chain, which are encased in lengths of old hose to cushion links. What is it? Well, it is a sandbox underneath; a climbing structure; a place to sun, to roll cars down, to roll down yourself or jump on...or you name it. Canvas is springy, soft.

Striped awning on a simple structure, right, can be a circus tent, a garage, a shade for tea parties, or perhaps the beginning of a lemonade stand. 10-foot, 4x4-inch posts are sunk into the ground, connect at top with 1-inch pipe. Awning arms are 1x3 inches; base panels are ¾-inch plywood. Awning is sewn from 42-inch-wide canvas to make a 6x6-foot roof. A pair of old sheets, thumbtacked in place, turn it into a tent for a day.

Play tower, left, can trigger all sorts of inventive play. A princess might be rescued, Comanches spotted from afar, a space rocket launched. 2x4s, ¾-inch plywood, and plywood climbing strips are all you need. Lower support at left houses a cabinet that stores toys. Circles cut into sides are good for climbing through.

Simple boxes with hand-holds cut into the ends can be used to form trains or to hold blocks; can be turned over for seats; and long after the children are grown will hold garage and garden supplies. Casters on bottoms and strong rope pulls will make it easier for very young children to use them.

It is hard to predict what mischief may occur to children, but some fairly obvious dangers can be avoided. When you provide cabinets and boxes or bins, remember that children like to crawl inside things to hide. Make sure that lids can be easily lifted from inside and that children do not have access to padlocks.

Add-on play structure, above, can start as a simple deck and playhouse. As your child grows, you can add the framework, using bolts or lag screws to make sure joints hold securely. Platforms can be made from 2x4s or ¾-inch plywood; playhouse section is of plywood. When your child climbs easily, add top platform and ladder, perhaps a rope to slide down. Boys and girls can enjoy these climbing gyms.

Four children play happily on swing set, above, which includes a slide, glider, two swings. Even if you are not handy with tools, you can install a manufactured unit like this at low cost for the play value it provides. Designating a special area as the children's play spot, in which they can be free to play as they will, helps them to respect the rest of the lot as reserved for adults. Do not plan a manicured lawn where children play; save that for garden or other adult areas. Keep the play area easy to maintain. Sand or gravel, enclosed with a low retaining wall, will blend with surroundings.

Borrow ideas from playgrounds

If you feel the need for more imaginative new ideas, visit a local playground to see the advances made in professional playground equipment. As an example, "tunnels" are popular and can be made of concrete pipe large enough for children to crawl through. You can substitute wooden hoops and canvas as a less durable but no less fun-filled version.

Include a sandbox in the play area

The most important piece of equipment for a children's play area is probably the sandbox. It has a hypnotic quality that invites long hours of quiet play out in the sunshine. Little children love to sift sand and make mud pies. Older boys and girls enjoy a box large enough to allow whole towns to be built, with miniature cars and small blocks to be used for buildings around their sand castles. And sophisticated 10- and 12-year-olds can sometimes study theories of irrigation and flood control if they are allowed to use the garden hose in the box.

Because it is so important, plan a box as large as your lot will allow, realizing that it

Even a tiny city lot can afford room for play. Here, a large square was left open in the concrete aggregate surface of terrace to provide a space for sand. Yard is completely fenced in, and door is fastened to keep children away from traffic. Sand can be swept back into square after play.

Big enough for a squadron of toddlers, the 18-foot seating and storage unit below effectively isolates children's area visually, yet keeps it within easy view of mother's sun chair. Seats lift up to reveal storage inside; are wide enough for sitting, for spreading out games, or for holding a whole collection of miniature cars.

will give years of play value. If you build it yourself, using weather-resistant exterior plywood or redwood, you can save money and probably achieve a better, sturdier sandbox.

Locate the sandbox where it will get plenty of morning sun, with shade at noon. If you lack trees or other natural shade, you can install a beach umbrella or construct a canvas screen. Plastic toys can usually be left right in the box, but you might need a storage box to keep metal cars and shovels shiny.

Place the box a little way from active toys like swings or seesaws, so gung-ho children do not disturb quiet "sandlubbers."

Special sandbox sand is more expensive than construction sand, but most children will enjoy the yard or two of construction sand you will need to buy for a large box just as much as the sandbox variety. The different sandboxes shown here demonstrate good things can come in many packages.

Providing water for play

Water play adds to the enjoyment a sandbox provides, and there are many ways to include provision for it in or near the sandbox. A tiny baby likes to splash around in a large dishpan on hot days. Later, a plastic pool, the right size for your youngsters, is another large piece of equipment well worth the investment; it provides hours of enjoyment. The younger the child, the more supervision of water play is of course required.

A wooden deck, concrete, gravel, or sand—all are suitable for the sandbox and pool area surface. These can be made attractive if the play area is designed to blend with the garden. Sturdy plants or shrubs can be planted near

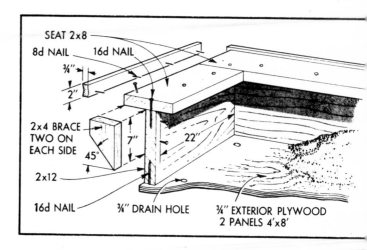

SEAT 2x8
8d NAIL   16d NAIL
¾"
2"
2x4 BRACE
TWO ON
EACH SIDE   7"   22"
45°
2x12
16d NAIL   ¾" DRAIN HOLE   ¾" EXTERIOR PLYWOOD
2 PANELS 4'x8'

Construction of sandbox at right is shown in sketch above. Floor is made of exterior-grade plywood for durability. Drain holes are important because they allow rainwater to escape and help to prevent warping. Braces support rim around sandbox so that it can be used for sitting. Sandbox is 8 feet square, allowing children to play the way toddlers do: together but separately, each busy with his activity.

Giant sandbox, right, is within view of many of the windows in house. The depth, 12 inches, makes it possible to fill it with a large amount of sand so children can make tunnels and get the feel of a beach. To provide shade, drill a hole through seating edge, stand a beach umbrella in the opening. Small plastic dishpan filled with water can be set on seating edge to provide makings for mud pies and cakes.

the sandbox or set in pots that roll near the pool, to help make the play area a decorative part of your home garden.

In planning a play area for your children, do not overlook the possibility of a small garden they can plant and tend. Whether they decide to grow vegetables or flowers, learning to be gardeners can be a meaningful experience for them, and may well inspire a hobby they will enjoy all their lives.

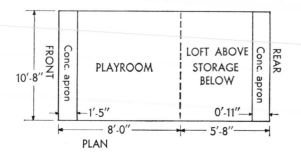

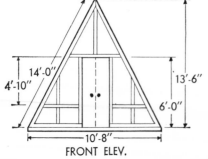

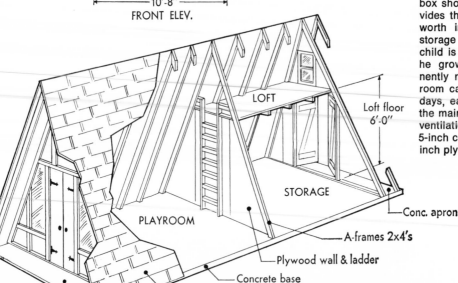

Plans, left, show simple construction of house. While this project is not inexpensive by any means, cost covers many years of enjoyment, and, like giant sandbox shown on the following pages, provides the kind of memorable play space worth investing money in. Loft above storage room can be used for naps when child is small, for overnight sleeping as he grows older. Ladder stays permanently mounted on plywood wall. Playroom can be especially useful on rainy days, easing the pressure on mother in the main house. Window in loft provides ventilation, view. Framing is anchored to 5-inch concrete base. Shingles cover ¾-inch plywood roof.

A toy that grows as your child does gives years of play value for your money. Simple gymnasium, above left, starts out with a pair of 4x4-inch posts, sunk in concrete. They stay for the life of the gym, but units attached to them change. For young child, attach triangular garage for toy trucks and climbing board. The center circle-in-a-square lets child swing, crawl, and dangle.

Second version of gymnasium, above right, has a ramp, another post, and crosspiece for use as a chinning bar. Climb up ramp, chin on bar, and then climb down a post to the ground. Square attached to right-hand post serves as a target for junior quarterbacks. As you add additional posts, be sure to use carriage bolts and lap the joints for extra strength. Chinning bar is a length of pipe.

When your child reaches basketball-and-baseball stage, version at left will serve several needs. Attach a basket to another, taller post for practicing basketball shots; add a strike panel for baseball target practice. Chinning bar is left in place to help steady posts. Later, child can adapt framework for individual needs, perhaps as a stand and tool rack for motor bike.

Simple Constructions to Enrich Your Life Outdoors

Whether you live in an area that permits year-round enjoyment of your garden, or where its use is confined to a few months of the year, you can increase the value and utility of your lot when you turn it into livable "rooms." Of course, an expanse of green lawn is pretty, but it takes lots of upkeep and is not half so usable as a yard that has been carefully planned to provide living spaces—areas for sitting, for dining, for vigorous outdoor play, for quiet meditation, for bright flowers, and shady nooks. Most of these activities take equipment and structures; these should blend with the house and with the surroundings. Perhaps you want more outdoor storage room; perhaps you need a place for serving drinks near the terrace. Whatever your project, it should suit your way of life; it should be structurally sound and should add to the architectural interest of your house, since it will survive some time.

Building useful, attractive projects

Even so simple a thing as a storage box for tennis rackets can be turned into a thing of beauty and double utility. Why not fashion a low sitting-bench that opens like a box? Take a cue from public parks and paint a chess-board on a simple plywood table-box; inside, store the checkers and chessmen and a few decks of cards. A sandbox bought in a store is nice—but for the same money you can make your own giant-size one, painted in bright colors, large enough for a whole neighborhood of kids. All you need are four long boards, braced at the corners with wooden triangles. You can nail additional boards hor-

Stylish western red cedar bench and planter unit, above, can be knocked down, moved to other locations. Four 1x12-inch boards, notched 3 inches from each end for half their width, slip together so notches meet, form box. Stringers, 1x4 inches, make legs 18 inches high. Strips, 1x1 inches, are nailed to leg supports to form seats.

Imaginative potting center, right, can be fitted into a sunny garden corner, or a greenhouse, or perhaps one end of a garage. Start with soil storage compartment, making sure it has a comfortable working height. Make it of ¾-inch exterior-grade plywood. The work surface and pot shelf are cleated at one end, supported by vertical boards at other. Pegboard panel is useful for holding garden tools.

◄ Seating and storage are provided in this graceful unit, left. End boxes have flip-tops, hide storage. Both are 2 feet square; one is 18 inches high to match bench; other is 24 inches high. Use 2x4-inch frames; cover with ½-inch rough plywood. Cleat them to a pair of 6-foot-long benches made of grooved exterior plywood. Smaller box (24x18x6 inches), topped with quarry tile, is an "end table." Using western cedar, exterior plywood, quarry tile, and outdoor paint ensures a long-lasting, durable project.

izontally onto the vertical sides to provide
seating and a place to display mud pies. Add
a beach umbrella and a small plastic pool,
and you have a toddler beach that will be
popular all summer long.

Creating projects with ease

Outdoor projects are fun for many reasons,
not the least of which is that you do not have
to be a master builder to create attractive and
practical furniture and equipment. Some principles are important; because the projects will
be used outdoors you have to anticipate some
problems. You will notice that many of these
projects use redwood strips rather than solid
redwood panels. This is to allow rain to fall
through instead of forming a puddle to warp
the wood. Cushions are covered in plastic or
canvas, and out-of-the-weather storage nooks
are provided for them in some cases. Bright
colors are more effective than intricate detail

Repairing a sling hammock is
not as difficult as you might
think, and it gives you a chance
to be artistic. You need 3 yards
of 36-inch-wide canvas. The
bright appliquéd squares are
cotton. Use your zigzag sewing
machine for the squares and to
sew a 3-inch seam at the foot
and a 15-inch seam at the head.
Nylon cord is used to attach
the canvas to the hammock
base. Metal eyelets are set into
the canvas.

This chaise longue is fashioned
of redwood slats, with a storage
platform underneath. It can be
used as a dining table when
it lies flat, or it can be raised
along its length to form a sofa
with a backrest. Use redwood
2x4s and 1x6s, rustproof nails,
and a handful of heavy butt
hinges. Support for chaise
longue swings on a lag bolt.
Notched plywood triangle
swings out to support the
lengthwise half when it becomes a sofa.

It will be hard to decide whether the grown-ups or the children in your family like this little house best. Protected from the wind or sudden showers, you can talk, sip drinks, or read. The frame is made from ¾-inch exterior-grade plywood and 2x4s. The top, sides, and bench tops are covered with strips of lattice molding; heavy rain will go through the slits so seats will not warp. The decorative edging, which results from extending the strips of lattice alternately—every other strip extends 6 inches out from perimeter of the house—will look even more decorative if plants or ivy are trained to climb up and over the house. Can you imagine this beside a pool, or tucked under an enormous golden willow tree? You could add niceties like a shelf, or canvas curtains to roll up or down.

in outdoor pieces; and because they are for outdoors, you can use a fairly large scale when you plan your project. That means that you will not need complicated tools; a hammer and nails or screws should suffice. You do have to figure your measurements accurately. Use the figures shown here as a guide. Much will depend on where you plan to install the project.

Outdoor storage possibilities

When your house needs extra storage room, why not look outside? The ingenious ideas shown here are just some of the many solutions for additional storage room you can find when you take a fresh look at your lot. One reason the ideas work is that they are planned to fit exactly the purposes for which they are designed. The owners decided what had to be stored, and planned the shelves, counters, bins, and closets to fit measurements and needs.

List the equipment you want to store, decide how much room you will need, and then be sure to include room for expansion. Within reason, you can plan ahead; the space that now houses the baby carriage will one day garage tricycles and then bicycles.

Freestanding unit, above left, has four doors which open to reveal many feet of practical storage room. It is planned for an avid gardener, with potting shelves, a place for the mower, lots of wall hooks for rakes, shovels, hand tools. The bulletin board ensures orderly disposition of routine garden tasks, so easily forgotten during lazy summer days. The roof is made of exterior-grade plywood. The framing and rafters are 2x4s; the decking is made of 2x3s, nailed with space between to allow rain to go through. The hinged doors open wide to give access to full contents of the cabinets. Large-equipment cabinets lock.

An inexpensive tool shed, left, uses an existing fence for one wall, and is really just two facing sets of shelves, with a roof overhead to join them. You could eliminate the roof to save money, but it does give the design unity and provides shade as well. The redwood slat roof could have been a translucent plastic panel. Gravel is an inexpensive flooring material and blends well with garden landscaping. Most of the storage area is made up of simple shelves, but one lockable cabinet, up high, is provided for storing poisons, insecticides, and so forth, high above the reach of children. Simple hooks or nails hold rakes and shovels.

FENCE

SHELVES   SHELVES

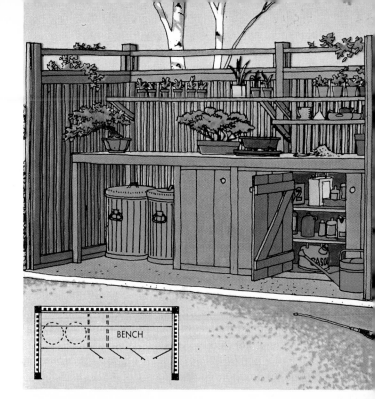

These classic cabinets turn a tiny terrace into a family room, because they can hold all the equipment you need for games or barbecue dining. Made of asbestos-cement board, they are durable and lockable, and can be painted in bright panels of color that are most attractive. The paper-towel holder and trash basket are stored in the cabinet. A unit like this can turn a corner of a porch into a mud room for children's coats, boots.

Another version of the unit, right, built against a fence, is a long counter that functions almost like a kitchen counter, with shelves above for plants, trash cans under the work surface, and under-counter storage for garden supplies. A roof could be added, making unit more versatile.

This unit, right, leans against a garage or carport to get the clutter out from under the wheels of the family car. Decorative supplies like potted plants, bright tools, and a colorful trash container are outside; inside, screened from view, is a cabinet for locked storage of tools. The bench is for sitting and dreaming about where the bulbs should be planted and is useful, too, as a work surface. The shelves are created by nailing crosspieces wherever you wish to the exposed framing. Small hand tools are hung against the exterior plywood wall panels.

Low-height unit, below, is ingeniously designed to take advantage of every inch of its space. Place it with low end facing prevailing storms. Broom-handle rod, placed crosswise, holds rakes and shovels above floor without requiring full-height cabinet. Concrete slab and ramp make it easy to roll mower and barrow into back cabinet. The doors swing up, hook in place while equipment is being rolled into storage area. Exterior shingles and exterior-grade plywood make this a long-lasting installation. Bright blue doors add beauty to the unit's utility; use outdoor paint.

Specialized Areas That Make Summertime Living Easier

Not all the rooms of a house need four walls, a roof, and a floor. A room for outdoor living, designed to take advantage of fresh air, sunshine, and garden greenery—or perhaps a magnificent view—is a welcome addition to any house. It offers the possibility of breakfast among the birds, with the early morning sunlight glittering on the coffee cups; a barbecue dinner at sunset; a midnight snack with candlelight, moonlight, and night sounds—or a quiet place to read on a lazy afternoon.

An outdoor room is a compromise between indoors and outdoors, between protection and exposure. It usually offers protection against direct sunlight and the eyes of neighbors and may protect against rain and light winds as well. It admits the smells and sounds of the outdoors and may even look like a part of the outdoors itself. It can be as simple as an awning attached to the side of a house, or it can be virtually a small house on its own.

Design considerations

An outdoor room can be a simple project or a major one, depending on its intended purpose and the resources available. It may have a floor—wood, brick, flagstone, or the like—or the natural ground may be used. If it is built adjacent to the house, one or more house walls may serve as walls for the new room. Other walls of a shaded outdoor room may be vine trellises, slat fences, plastic panels, or

This unusual and attractive shelter, suggestive of Moorish arches, is simple to assemble. Vaulted panels of exterior-grade plywood are supported by rigid frames of 4-inch steel H-columns on 8-foot centers. Screens are deck gratings.

A Japanese-style screened ▶ house offers both shade and protection from insects. This one is 8x20 feet, supported on six precast concrete posts sunk below the frost line. The framing is of 2x4s and 2x6s, with insect screening on three sides; the fourth, solid wall is of plywood and includes several storage cabinets. Floor joists are placed every 2 feet, with 2x6 blocking between.

This elegant and colorful roof is very simple to make. Start with a pair of vertical columns (each made of two 2x6s), each supporting an overhanging beam (made of two 2x8s). Attach a 2x8 outrigger to the ends of the beams, and add two transverse lattices of 2x4s and 1-inch planking. Then anchor bright canvas strips to the outrigger, weave them alternately over and under the transverses, and anchor them to the house. The colors of the roof can be echoed in the furniture.

Corrugated plastic protects against rain and direct sunlight, creating a soft, shadowless glow. The plastic panels are laid on an egg-crate structure of redwood 2x8s and 2x4s, which is supported by pipes attached to the walls of the patio. The light-colored cedar decking has been protected against spilled drinks and barbecue stains by a clear sealer such as spar varnish. Built-in brick planters, with their bright flowers, provide color.

tall hedges; and one or more walls may be simply left open. Shade and protection from rain may be provided by some of the same materials; other possibilities are fabric or plastic awnings, various kinds of special roof construction, or a good-sized tree.

Determining the room's placement

First, the site of the new room must be decided upon. Specifically, will it adjoin the present house—having one or more walls in common with it—or not? The main advantages of an adjoining room are convenience of use and simplicity of construction. The house can provide electricity, running water, a telephone, and such other facilities as a kitchen and a bathroom. These considerations are particularly important if the new room is expected to be used much for entertaining, with the attendant activities of serving and cleanup.

From a construction viewpoint, a site adjoining the main house offers the advantage of simplicity. One wall at least is already in place—perhaps no more than an awning, a hedge, and some garden furniture will be needed to complete the project. If a more ambitious project is planned, the easy availability of house power, water, and storage facilities will still make an important difference in the ease of construction.

On the other hand, if the planned room is intended to take advantage of a particular view, or the mood of an isolated spot in the woods, it will have to be sited accordingly. As long as the construction is kept simple and practical, the sacrifice in convenience may be more than paid for by the beauty and seclusion of the chosen location.

Sometimes the design of an outdoor room will be planned around an existing shade tree. If such a tree is available, it may make an excellent starting point for an outdoor room— what better way of providing both shade and atmosphere than by building the room around a tree?

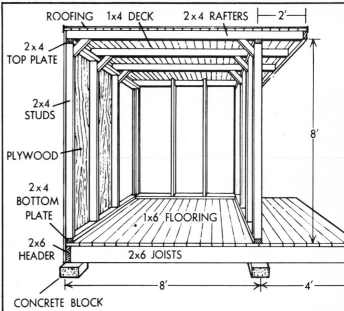

This little house can be a shady shelter in a backyard, or a solitary retreat in the woods. The front can be left open, or covered with insect screening, split bamboo screening, a weatherproof canvas awning, or the like (where birds, rabbits, squirrels, and similar invaders may be expected, some kind of screening is mandatory). To protect the wood from ground moisture, use concrete or cinder blocks under the floor joists (tree stumps, properly treated with preservative, may be used if conveniently located). The rear wall should be of exterior-grade plywood: more expensive, but worth it for its long-term durability in all weather.

Weatherizing the room

An outdoor room is open to the air and yet protected against climatic extremes. After the site has been chosen, the next question to be decided is how much protection will be needed, and against what? Some of the considerations here are sun, rain, wind, insects, other kinds of pests, and possibly the eyes of neighbors.

The room must admit enough sun to seem outdoors, and at the same time provide enough shade for comfort. Depending on location, that may mean no roof at all, a partial roof, or a roof over the whole area; and the roof may be either solid or partially open—like a flower-covered trellis—to provide light-dappled shade. The same considerations apply to walls, both in placement and in construction.

Should the shelter be windproof? That will depend on several factors, notably its intended use, its location, and the kind of winds that may be expected. An open, shady pavilion in a warm climate may be designed to take advantage of any cooling breezes that pass by; while a hillside barbecue area may need to be protected against the chilly winds of late afternoon. Needless to say, a windproof wall is generally a more ambitious construction project than a wall which merely provides shade.

How much protection against rain is required? It is very pleasant to sit outdoors, protected from direct rainfall, and enjoy the sounds and smells of a summer shower; but that calls for a waterproof roof, and possibly some protection against windborne spray from

This beautiful garden room was once a useless area between the house and a street-side garage. With the existing shade tree as a suggestive starting point, the area was converted into a secluded outdoor retreat. The overhead grid supports a vine which screens the view of taller houses on either side, as well as providing some shade and contributing to the garden effect. A profusion of hanging plant baskets, as well as several small trees and bushes in tubs, intensifies the garden atmosphere while taking very little space.

the sides. It may be more practical to plan on waiting out such storms inside the house.

If the outdoor room must be screened against insects, it will have to be enclosed (or at least closable) on all four sides. This limits freedom of design, making it almost impossible to achieve the open effect of some other types of shelters. However, it also offers protection against other small marauders, such as birds, rabbits, field mice, and the like—an important advantage in some locations.

Where sidewalks, roadways, or neighboring houses are immediately adjacent to the planned outdoor shade area, some kind of fence or screen must be provided to ensure privacy. A plain wooden fence may be used, or a fence of translucent plastic panels in a wood frame —or perhaps a densely grown hedge. If near-

Here are three different ways of providing shade without trapping hot air. The louvered roof permits easy vertical airflow, while blocking most of the sun's rays except when it is directly overhead (the width and spacing of the boards used determines the sun-stopping power—it is even possible to stop the sun at noon, if desired, by mounting the boards on a slant). The slat fence around three sides of the roofed area permits the free passage of cooling breezes; and the oversize umbrella, being nearly flat, traps almost no air under it.

This lightly shaded barbecue area and outdoor family room was once an asphalt parking area. The various elements are nicely coordinated to provide a relaxing atmosphere: the textures of brick, wood, and gravel— set off by the patches of greenery—blend well, and thus soften the lines of the simple geometric design. The design is efficient and attractive: sliding glass doors provide easy access to house, and barbecue, with its wide counter, is a neat and appropriate addition to the chimney.

by two-story houses overlook the area, an overhead trellis covered with vines provides privacy, shade, and a garden atmosphere.

Thus the basic design of an outdoor room depends on the uses to which it will be put, the kinds of protection needed, and the resources available.

Before: A comfortable but rather ordinary-looking older house, with a separate garage, above. A large tree offers shade.

After: Here the garage has been moved up next to the house, at right, creating an L shape. The owners like to entertain large groups of friends, so they designed a giant deck that would fit into the L and extend around one side of the house and part of another. The deck is supported on short columns, which raise it to the same height as the home's first floor. Sliding glass doors provide access from the kitchen and from two sides of the family room for free and easy circulation. The shade tree was carefully preserved throughout the renovation: a cutout was left in the decking to accomodate the trunk, and the house and garage now share its shade with the new party deck. The newly planted shrubs along the edge of the deck will hide the area under the deck.

Making the most of available space

Where land costs are high, houses close together, and additional space nonexistent, a private outdoor room can be created only by converting space from some other use. Suburbanites with limited land can profit from the imaginative techniques of city dwellers, who have long been adept at creating vest-pocket gardens in unlikely places. A backyard, a dead area between house and garage, an awkward slope or rocky area—any of these can be transformed, by the judicious use of flooring, fencing, roofing, and planting, into an attractive area for outdoor living.

If the ground is not level, a raised floor can make it so; or it may be terraced into several level areas, making an interesting design feature out of a liability. Gardenlike effects can be created, at a minimum cost in floor space, by hanging pots of plants from overhead beams, planting small trees or bushes in tubs, and training vines over walls.

Where space is a problem, a well-considered layout can make the outdoor room seem larger than it really is. A small area can be planned to have several levels, to have several uses, even to include a pool, as long as the scale is appropriate to the size of the space. A slightly raised flagstone patio might overlook a grassy lawn; a cedar deck might lead down to a raked sand and pebble yard; a brick dining terrace might be a few steps above a patio of concrete aggregate. The different levels lead naturally to differences in use, and the variety increases the apparent size of the area.

Another way to differentiate areas is by using different flooring materials. Pebbled areas can alternate with brick or flagstones, aggregate pathways can divide a grassy area, or vice versa, narrow planters can divide an aggregate floor—and the like. Plants and small trees in tubs, or ground-planted bushes, can also separate areas—and perhaps provide a bit of shade as well.

Too much differentiation of areas should be avoided, however, since it can produce a crowded, uncomfortable effect. This can also occur if the outdoor room is asked to serve too many different purposes. One way to avoid such an overbusy atmosphere is to coordinate the various areas by means of a repeated design motif: a distinctive shape, material, or texture, which will suggest, by its repetition, the unity of design of the outdoor room.

The windows of the living room, the master bedroom, and the kitchen all overlook a small outdoor area carefully planned to provide a beautiful year-round view, as well as outdoor living space. Easy access from both kitchen and living room makes outdoor dining and entertaining a pleasure. A brick terrace leads down a couple of steps to a larger patio, floored with pebble-textured aggregate concrete. Two brick planters were built around existing trees, and the design of these two is echoed by two other planters and a small pool. To ensure privacy, a high cedar fence masks three sides of the area.

Accessories and trim

In a small outdoor room which is planned to have extensive plantings, the greenery can be used to give an illusion of space. Borrow a trick from the Japanese, who are practised artists in the use of limited space: plant for perspective. Place taller plants near the front of the planted area, with smaller ones behind them: this will create an effect of receding space, suggesting visual distance without adding an inch of floor space.

Imaginative use of lighting can also control the size of an outdoor room, at least at night. Brightly lit areas tend to seem larger and freer than dim ones. If each use-area has plenty of electric light, controlled by its own inexpensive solid-state dimmer, the areas can be selectively expanded and contracted by simply changing the lighting.

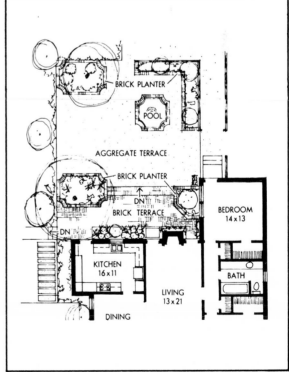

How to Choose and Use the Right Materials for Your Painting Projects

Today's do-it-yourself painter has it made. During the past decade, paint technology has benefited from a number of notable advances, so that painting the home inside or out can be quicker and easier than ever, with better results and a much greater variety of possible colors and surface finishes.

Perhaps the most important advances have occurred in the field of the so-called latex paints. A few years ago, these easy-cleanup, water-thinned paints could not offer much hiding power. Today they do, and they are available even in glossy finishes.

There are other paints that old-time painters would never have dreamed possible. Who would have believed, for example, that one day you could apply paint to a porcelain sink and have it adhere for years?

More, there is, figuratively speaking, an infinity of colors. You can give your color imagination free rein—you can find the most arresting purples and oranges or the subtlest possible pastel pinks and yellows. If you cannot mix the color yourself, or if you cannot buy it in ready-mix form, your dealer will custom-mix it for you at a very modest charge.

All you need to take advantage of products on the market is know-how. And that is what you will find on the pages that follow: the complete story of preparing and painting the inside and outside of your home. Before you know it, you will be turning out a job that is equal to that which a professional can do, and yours will have the special ingredient of personal concern. In other words, you can easily manage a paint job that will do you, and your house, proud.

Room at left shows what can be done with leftover paint—and savings achieved at the same time. Segments of closet door were painted with small amounts of paints, unused in other rooms, which otherwise would have been discarded. Think of leftover paints in terms of their ability to serve as accent colors. One wall? Stair railing? Cabinets? Doors? Woodwork?

Visualize this room with all-white walls and you will see ▶ how much the choice of a bright orange color scheme and the addition of the giant graphic enliven and unify it. The graphic was painted in deck enamel for a wet look.

Equipment

You may be able to turn a screw with a bargain-basement screwdriver, but top-notch painting simply cannot be done with inferior tools. Whatever you buy, let *quality* be your watchword. Not only will you do a better job, but it will be very much easier. And the tools will be around for years—a *real* bargain.

Brushes

It used to be that a "quality" brush meant one with genuine animal-hair bristles. This is no longer true. Now brushes with synthetic bristles such as nylon will serve you perfectly well inside or outside the house. They can be used with either latex (water-thinned) or oil-base (solvent-thinned) paint. One caution: if you buy an animal-hair brush, do not use it with latex.

1. A brush caked with paint is a candidate for a good brush cleaner. The water-wash type works very well. First, move bristles back and forth in the cleaner, letting it penetrate completely. From time to time, check to see if paint is softening. When it is about the consistency of jelly, it is ready for removal.

2. Removal is a chore for a brush, comb, other toothed item. Work from the ferrule (metal band around brush) out, stripping off the paint in small globs. Do not tug hard, or you might pull out bristles. In other words, let the cleaner remove the paint. If soaking is called for, hang brush by wire, so bristles do not touch can.

Wild bristles

Dried paint

Heeled up

3. After all paint has been removed, wash brush in warm—not hot—soapy water, gently kneading the bristles with your fingers. Rinse in clear warm water, wrap with foil or oilcloth, and hang up or lay flat to dry. Throughout the process, follow directions on brush-cleaner label, paying special attention to safety precautions.

Brushes here are victims of poor cleaning procedures. One at left was allowed to soak in solvent too long; middle brush was not cleaned after use; one at right was not cleaned thoroughly. The two brushes with paint in them can be restored with brush cleaner. Wild-bristle one has had it; is good only for dusting.

When new, a poor-quality brush can look just as good as one of fine quality. But there are ways to tell the difference. First, feel the bristles. If they are silky smooth, you have a good brush; bristles of a poor one will be coarse. Also, grasp the bristles in your hand. A good brush will feel full; a poor one feels light.

Yet another way—the classic way—of testing a brush for quality is to see whether its bristle ends are flagged—split—as shown. The more flags, the better the brush. But beware of false flags: bristles that have been chopped to look as if they are flagged. Look closely and you will see they are not split.

It is a good idea to break in a new brush before using it. For a nylon- or other synthetic-bristle brush, merely draw it across a rough surface to release any loose bristles. If you have bought a natural-bristle brush, soak it in raw linseed oil for 24 hours; remove oil with turpentine; rub brush on rough surface.

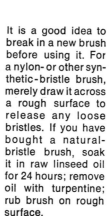

Besides having loose bristles, a new brush may have some bent ones. These can be annoying when you are painting. Remove them one at a time. Simply pull each down against the ferrule, as shown at left.

There is a brush to answer every painting need. Left to right: a 4-inch brush for large areas, such as walls; an angled sash brush for windows; a 2-incher for woodwork; super-tiny 1-incher for unsteady hands. Brush at top is natural-bristle 2-incher, good for applying clear finishes. It is best to reserve the clear-finish brush for this job alone. Colored paint in bristles could run out.

It is best to buy a few brushes in different sizes so that you can have greater manual control of the brush as well as better coverage when you paint particular areas. The same sizes are recommended for both exterior and interior painting: a 4- or 5-inch brush (the latter only if you have a strong arm) for painting large, unadorned areas, such as walls and house siding; a 2½- or 3-inch brush for woodwork and "cutting in" (painting places where a roller cannot fit); and a 1½- or 2-incher for window frames and mullions.

You can check several things to determine if a brush is good. But as accurate a criterion as any is price: good brushes cost three and four times as much as poor ones. You should pay at least $6 for the 4- or 5-inch brush, $4 for the 2½- or 3-inch brush, and $3 for the smallest. You will not regret it.

Choosing and using rollers

Perhaps no other thing—new paints included—has spurred on do-it-yourself house painting so much as has the roller. With it, the inexperienced painter can get results that are professional in every way.

Inside the house, rollers are better for painting large, flat areas, like walls and ceilings, and brushes are better for doing woodwork and places the roller cannot fit, like room corners.

Actually, when we talk about rollers for walls and ceilings, we mean walls and ceilings of bedrooms, living rooms, places where you will apply flat (non-glossy) paint. A 4-inch brush is recommended for applying enamel (glossy) paint in kitchen and bath. You could use a mohair—short-bristled—roller for enamel, but the finish achieved tends to be less smooth. It may be dimpled all over, have an orange-peel texture, and be less shiny than brush-applied enamel.

Rollers are available in 7- and 9-inch lengths and in a variety of fabrics, mostly synthetic. You need not concern yourself about length or fabric. Just tell the dealer that you want rollers for walls and ceilings. But do be concerned about price. Spend at least $1.50 for each. For this, you will get quality rollers that will make the job go faster and look better and will keep you from giving up in despair. If you are wise, you will resist the temptation to buy those throw-away rollers that come, usually, two to a plastic bag.

Length is immaterial. Most people, even women, seem to find the 9-inch as easy to handle as the 7-inch size.

Along with the roller (or cover or sleeve, as it is also called) you need a pan and a handle to which the roller attaches. Buy good quality here,

When you are using a roller, let the paint do the work for you. Run your roller into a half-filled pan, submerging it. When it is saturated, draw it out of the paint and roll it on grated part of pan to remove excess. Fully loaded roller should be heavy with paint, but not hold so much it drips. Handy trick: keep cutting-in brush in pan. It is right there when you need it.

First step in painting a room is to cut in around windows, woodwork, room corners—wherever the roller will not go. Make your cut lines about an inch wide. Roll adjacent area. When roller is almost out of paint, roll next to woodwork, or whatever, covering as much of cut line as possible. Brush leaves a different texture, so what you do not cover with the roller will show up.

New breed of rollers includes this tiny one designed for trim work. Unlike most rollers the one shown above is faster than a brush for painting insides of closets, but it leaves slight marks where paint trails off roller ends. If this does not matter, you can use it.

After cutting in around woodwork with a brush, roll paint as close to the trim as possible in order to ensure a consistent finish—the brush and the roller will render different textures. Some rollers are equipped with guards to protect trim from inadvertent smears. In any case, the roller should not be overloaded when you paint close to woodwork; distribute some of the fresh paint on flat wall so you will have a partially dry roller for close work.

Picture at left shows that you can paint "any old way" and not have to worry about lap marks. It is important, however, to remove the fine lines of paint that come off the ends of a roller—even a good roller. These lines would dry a slightly darker color than rest of finish and, of course, be visible.

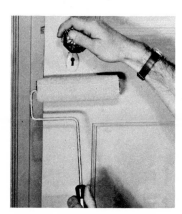

Roller can be used to paint a door. First, cut in molding and raised portions around doorknob; then paint flat areas with roller, going as close to molding as you can. Paint door edges before doing larger flat areas, using light strokes. Pressure will squeeze the paint out of roller ends.

too. Ask for a tube-type handle. The tube may be formed by wires or actually be a metal tube. Either way, it is easy to slip the roller on and off. Avoid the kind of handle that has a rod and a pair of wing nuts.

If you are planning to paint more than one room, it is a good idea to buy two complete roller outfits—two rollers, two handles, and two pans. Then, when you switch from one paint to another, you do not have to stop to clean your first outfit. Just immerse the roller in paint —so it does not dry out—and proceed with your fresh outfit.

Equipment for exterior painting

Rollers are not generally desirable for exterior painting. While they might seem faster than brushes, they are not. House siding—clapboard, shingles, shakes, and so forth—has so many areas to paint that are inaccessible to a roller that switching back and forth between roller and brush is really time consuming. In addition, brush and roller textures are different—and the differences show up all too plainly.

There are two main exceptions to the rule. The first is masonry—brick, block, stucco, cement, cement walls, walkways, and so on. Here the surface is usually large and recess-free, but it is also very rough. A brush has great difficulty coping with all the tiny hills and valleys and suffers a little every time it tries (so does your arm). On such rough materials, use a lambskin roller with a ¾-inch nap (fabric). When they are wet with paint, the long fibers find their way easily—with only a pass or two of the roller— into all the nooks and crannies.

The other exception is chain link fencing. This has its own kind of hills and valleys, which are best handled by a long-nap roller.

Roller techniques

Using a roller is simple. Paint ceilings in strips about 3 feet wide, going across the width of the room. As you go, cut in the wall-ceiling joint with a brush or small trimmer roller. Roll only an area that can be easily seen and easily reached at one time. Use plenty of paint, applying it in one direction with your first strokes, then criss-crossing, then making smoothing strokes in the same direction as the first ones. Do not worry about all the strokes being straight. They can go any way, and the paint will still dry without lap marks. When you finish a strip, be sure to overlap the next strip on it, so that wet paint is always going into wet paint. If you apply wet paint over nonabsorbent dry paint, permanent lap marks will result.

Paint walls from top to bottom in 3- or 4-foot-wide strips, cutting in the corresponding section of baseboard as you go—not after all walls are finished. Roll on paint with diagonal strokes; then smooth it with straight up-and-down strokes. If you have to interrupt the painting, stop at a corner, not in the middle of a wall.

As soon as you have finished painting a strip on either the wall or the ceiling, check to see if there are any missed or uneven spots, and touch them up immediately.

In recent years, new rollers have been introduced in many sizes and shapes, including some that look like doughnuts and saucers. Their common purpose is to replace or augment brushes. However, if you stick with standard rollers and brushes, you will be well-equipped for any painting.

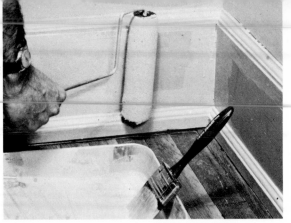

If baseboard is wide enough, roller can be used to paint it. First, cut in baseboard at top and bottom with a brush; then fill in between cut lines with strokes of roller, as shown above. Roller is also good for painting insides of closets. Cut in the corners with a brush; then use roller.

To paint ceilings without using a stepladder, extend the roller with the gadget shown here. A metal collar, tightened with a screwdriver, grips both the handle and the extension rod. Unless you intend to have switch plates match your walls, be sure to remove them before painting.

A surprising amount of paint can accumulate in a roller during a job. Then it seems to take forever to wash it. A trick to shorten the task is shown above. Run your scraper or painting stick down the fabric, squeezing out the paint into a can. If the fabric on the roller is of good quality, it can withstand this.

Sprayers

Spray guns and cans can be useful additions to your painting arsenal, as long as you recognize their limitations and handle them properly.

Usually, it is not practical to paint house siding with a gun (trim definitely cannot be done). A gun of the size required throws out a tremendous volume of paint in mist form, and unless your house is isolated, some of it is almost sure to float onto a neighbor's property. Indeed, paint will drift around your own property—perhaps landing on an automobile nearby or on your favorite rosebush. More than that, a gun this big might cost $200 or more.

Of course, you could try painting the siding on a dead-calm day—with nothing guaranteed—but you still would have to mask doors and windows and everything else you did not want paint to fall on. This is a tedious, time-consuming process. It is sensible to avoid it.

The same problem—mist—persists to a lesser degree (because you use a much smaller gun)

Paint for this big spray outfit can be contained in feed tank, left, or gun/container, center. You could use this rig to paint your house.

when you are spray-painting furniture and the like outdoors. However, if you choose a calm day and mask the immediate area, you should not have any trouble.

Above all, never use a spray gun indoors except under controlled conditions. It is simply too big. Not only will the mist get on everything, but the vapors will constitute a fire hazard. If you can build, in your basement or workshop, a cardboard booth, vented to the outside with an exhaust fan, you can spray paint indoors.

For indoor work—appliances, furniture, and so on—a spray can should be adequate. These little cans—just like the guns—produce a very smooth finish, smoother than will any other applicator. But either work with the can in the aforementioned booth or take great care in masking. Cover everything in the room where you are painting, plus openings to other rooms. Best bet here is cheap plastic dropcloths, taped—all around—over furniture, doorways, etc. And be sure to open the windows. If you wish, you can buy a cheap respirator, but wearing one is not absolutely necessary.

Advantages of spray guns

In addition to assuring an ultra-smooth finish, a spray gun can paint things that defy a brush or roller. Prime example is a picket fence. Its grooves and recesses murder a brush and are too small for a roller to penetrate. Spray mist, however, easily finds its way into them.

Other easy jobs for a spray gun: other types of fencing, shutters, and masonry.

A further advantage of owning a spray gun is that you can spray liquids other than paint, such as insecticides, fertilizers, mothproofers, and carpet and upholstery detergents.

If you think you would like to have a spray-gun outfit, you should know about its many parts. Every gun has a compressor—with or without a motor—which supplies the air that mixes with the paint to form the mist; a paint container, on the gun or separate; and a hose. In selecting a gun, you must consider these

Internal-mix nozzle, left, mixes air and liquid inside the nozzle; external-mix type mixes them outside. Internal is best suited for spraying house paints, enamels, and multi-color paints. External is a general-purpose unit suitable for all common materials and fast-drying ones. Whatever nozzle you use, always clean it right after use.

When working indoors with spray gun or can, protect everything—airborne spray can land where you do not want it. Cover furniture, close doors, tape sheets over open doorways leading to other rooms. Also, ventilate room well; spray can be noxious. Good trick for catching over-spray is to hold a piece of cardboard behind item.

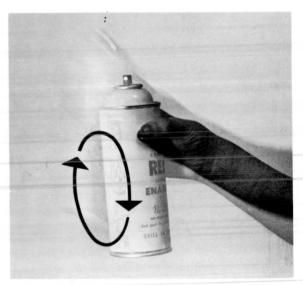

Aerosol spray cans are most convenient for small jobs. They eliminate the bother of mixing a batch of paint, and waste is minimal. You can buy all kinds of paint in aerosol form, including enamel, flat, and epoxy, and in many colors. Stains, varnish, shellac, sealer, primer, and a variety of other finishes are also available. Large paint stores usually carry a fairly complete line.

Before using spray can, shake it vigorously, as shown above. If you are working with colored paint, you will hear a steel ball clacking around inside the container. When you hear it rolling on the bottom, paint is mixed. Every few minutes while you are spraying, shake to keep paint mixed. After use, immediately clean spray head by turning can upside down, spraying until clear.

Always keep spray gun or can square to surface being painted and a steady distance away, anywhere from 6 to 10 inches. Start spraying off to the left of the object, then sweep spray across it without stopping. Stop only when you have completely cleared the object. Before spraying, it is a good idea to practice on a piece of cardboard. One does not acquire the knack instantly.

After making one pass, return and make another, overlapping about half of the first band of paint. Proceed like this, moving from top to bottom of object. Spraying on two thin coats is better than trying to do the painting with one application. Allow sufficient drying time between coats. Some paints, such as epoxy, require sanding of first coat.

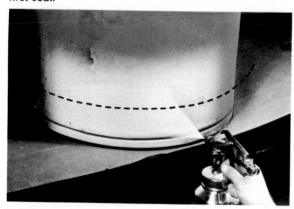

Follow essentially the same procedure for painting round objects as flat ones. Keep the gun moving steadily and at an even distance from the surface. Dotted line shows proper path. If surface—round or flat—has recesses or hard-to-paint places, do these first. Observe safety precautions when using sprayers. Most important, never spray where there is danger of fire.

things and also the gun's nozzle—whether paint and air are mixed externally or internally—and whether or not it is a bleeder (constantly letting out air while you paint) or a nonbleeder.

After determining what items you will be painting, what kind of paint you will use, and how often you will paint, combine the spray-gun features that will serve you best, and buy that equipment. For a very active do-it-yourselfer, a unit composed of a 1/3-horsepower compressor, 25 feet of air hose, and a bleeder-type, internal-mix spray gun with a self-contained paint container should be adequate. You cannot paint your barn with it, but it will manage all kinds of fencing and do a good finishing job on anything your workshop produces. Cost ranges from $100 to $150. Instead of buying, remember, you can always rent an outfit.

SAG

If sprayer is held too long on an area, paint piles up and sags. Cure: wipe away sag with your palm (a cloth could leave lint) while the paint is wet, and spray spot with two light, quick coats.

RUN

Run is result of a sag that gave way. Use the cure described above. If the paint consistently sags or runs, you have not yet mastered the speed at which to apply it.

HOLIDAY

"Holiday" is the professional painter's name for a missed spot. Correct the mistake with two light coats. Remember: sprayer must be moving as paint is applied.

ORANGE-PEELING

"Orange-peeling" is the descriptive term for applied paint that has the texture of orange skin. Too-thick paint or too much air pressure can be the cause. Solution: wipe off the paint and start over.

Which Paint for You?

While distinctions within distinctions can be made about paints, when you boil them down, you have a choice between two types for the interior or exterior of your home: latex (or emulsion) paint, which is water-thinned, and oil-base, which is solvent-thinned. Both are available in flat finishes for large areas, such as walls and siding, and in glosses for woodwork (or trim, as outside woodwork is called).

While there may be some disagreement on their relative merits, the fact seems to be that both water-base and oil-base paints have their virtues, one being more suitable than the other, depending upon the application. These considerations are discussed in other sections of this article.

It is just as important, after you have chosen the right paint for the job, to be sure that the quality of the paint is good. Paint of good quality covers more area (perhaps twice as much) as the same amount of poor paint; it covers the surface more evenly and with better concealment, fades less, and goes on more easily. And it will look better than cheap paint—its colors will be richer and its reflection of light subtler.

Fortunately, there is nothing complicated about getting a good paint. The rule of thumb, as for any other purchase, is that you get what you pay for; the rule applies with special force if you are buying something about which you have no expert knowledge. Although good paint is made by small manufacturers, the inexperienced painter will probably feel safest if he relies on the top-quality lines of well-known manufacturers. The only valid bargain in paints is to buy recognized brands when the paint dealer has a sale.

Creating the finish you want

If you want glossy finish on siding, choose an oil-base paint; for an almost-flat finish, choose latex. For a fairly high-gloss finish on woodwork, get oil-base; for less gloss, use latex trim.

One big question do-it-yourselfers ask is: "How many coats should I use?" Usually, two situations call for a two-coat interior or exterior job: (1) when the existing surface is in very poor condition—inside, where many, many patches must be made; or outside, where much peeling paint must be removed; (2) where a drastic color change is being made. The rule here is that any light color can be covered with one coat of any dark color; but dark colors normally cannot be covered by one coat of a lighter color. If colors are close in tone (say, white and yellow, or cream and off-white, or green and blue), you probably can get by with one coat, even though you are going from dark to lighter. Do not believe "one coat covers all" claims about paint. If you are changing from a really dark color to a lighter one, 99 out of 100 paints cannot cover in one coat—and one coat of the hundredth paint is likely to cost you as much as two coats of any of the other 99.

If two coats will be required, ask your dealer about primers. These are formulated to serve well as a base for your finish coat—and they are cheaper. But buy top-of-the-line primer, too.

No matter what paint you buy, follow the manufacturer's directions for using it. Not doing so is the most common reason for failure. People do not read the label, and the painting is a disaster. Cases have been recorded, in fact, of people using turpentine or some other solvent to thin paint when water was called for. That is like using salt to sweeten coffee. The manufacturer's label tells you when to use the paint, where, how much, how to mix it, how to prepare surfaces for it, and what applicator to use. If you follow directions, painting should be not only problem-free, but easier.

Special-purpose paints

The research activity of paint companies in recent years makes beavers look lazy. The result is not only improvement in standard paints, but the creation of several special-purpose ones. Here is a roundup of some that are useful.

■ Epoxy: Modern epoxy paints provide one of the toughest finishes available. They have fantastic gripping power, making it possible to paint formerly unpaintable materials like tile, porcelain, and plastic laminates.

While great, epoxies are by no means foolproof. In fact, many people report poor results. Analysis of epoxy failures shows different reasons for them, the foremost being inadequate preparation of surfaces.

The surface must be not just fairly clean, it must be absolutely clean. Surface soil, grease, and the like must go; so must ground-in soil. When painting bathroom or kitchen fixtures, for example, you must first scrub with detergent, then rub, rub, rub with a paste of powdered pumice (sold at paint stores) and water. This acts like an old-time scouring powder. After the scouring, the surface must be thoroughly rinsed and completely dried.

Epoxies will also take hold on wood, fiber glass, most plastics, and other nonporous surfaces.

Before applying epoxy to a painted surface, test to see if it lifts up the old paint. Just dab a little epoxy on an out-of-the-way spot. Remember that the epoxy in this case is not adhering to the surface, but only to the old paint. Some brands of epoxy specify that the old paint must come off. Others specify special primers.

Another factor when using epoxy is temperature: adequate warmth is necessary for the paint to harden properly. Both the epoxy and the surface to be painted should be between 60 and 80 degrees.

The really good epoxies are two-component—the paint comes in two cans, which you mix just before use. Since the good variety hardens by chemical action rather than by drying, mixing properly is very important. Unless it is thoroughly blended, hardening will be partial on some sections. Follow label directions precisely. Usually you are instructed to stir the paint for 3 or 4 minutes, let it stand 20 minutes, then stir again.

Be sure to apply epoxy quickly. The "pot life" of most is only about two hours. After that, it hardens and is useless.

Epoxy is expensive. It may cost $5 a quart. Limit its use to small items.

■ Texture, sand-finish flats: When ceilings or walls are basically sound but have many hairline cracks or little bumpy patches that would require great effort to fix, texture paints can cover over—hide—the imperfections. These paints have a heavy, jellylike consistency and are applied with a brush or roller. While the paint is still wet, you can texture its yielding surface with a brush, roller, sponge, whisk broom, or wad of crushed paper.

Sand-finish flats have a gritty material suspended in them. They do not offer quite the hiding power of texture paints, but the sandy finish does hide better than regular paint. They can be put on with a brush or roller. For either of these types of paint, check the label for coverage. It may be as small as 25 square feet to the gallon. However, these paints are much cheaper than conventional ones.

■ Masonry paints: Oil-base paint is not the best kind for stucco, brick, and other masonry. Masonry, even if it is not new, exudes alkali, which oil-base paint does not stand up to well.

Latex paints are excellent for masonry. They withstand alkali well, and also handle better than oil-base the moisture masonry is prone to. But, if you want to save a good bit of money, use cement-base paint. This comes as a powder, which you mix with water. Drawbacks: it can be used only on unpainted masonry. It is messy, and the surface must be spray-hosed before painting.

■ Screen enamel: A thin paint designed to envelop screen wire without filling the openings between wires. It is best applied as a spray, with a piece of carpet, or with a carpetlike applicator you can buy. Time-saving trick: spray through several screens at the same time.

■ Porch and deck enamel: A high-gloss paint with extra resistance to abrasion. It can be used

LATEX

CLEAR
EPOXY

SEMIGLOSS
ENAMEL

GLOSS
ENAMEL

WATERPROOFING
WATER BASE

URETHANE

EPOXY

SILICONE

MASONRY COATINGS

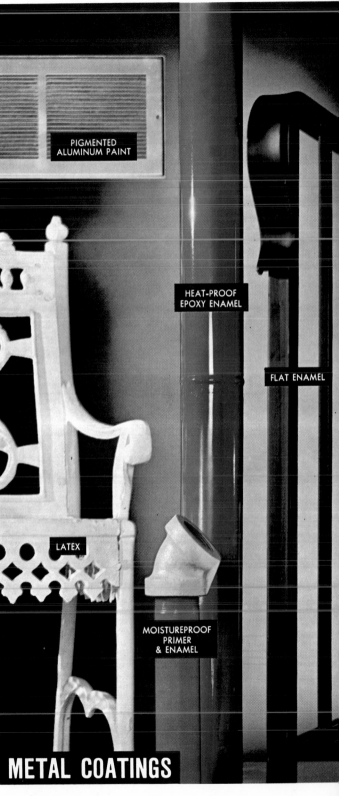

PIGMENTED
ALUMINUM PAINT

HEAT-PROOF
EPOXY ENAMEL

FLAT ENAMEL

LATEX

MOISTUREPROOF
PRIMER
& ENAMEL

METAL COATINGS

on floors, wood decks, and wood steps. You can also paint linoleum with it, but not rubber or asphalt tile. The enamel will dissolve these materials.

■ Flat black: Made specifically for iron grillwork. It dries to total flatness—no reflection of light—resembling real wrought iron. Use it on all kinds of ironwork—lawn furniture, stair railings, fences, and so on. The paint comes either in regular form or in convenient aerosol spray cans.

■ Heat-resistant paint: This can stand extremely high temperatures without peeling, fading, being affected in any way. Use it on heaters, radiators, trash burners, stoves, pipes, and the like. If you cannot find it in regular paint stores, try automotive paint stores. It is most commonly available in spray cans. (Note: heat-resistant paint should not be confused with fire-retardant paint.)

To find out what else is on the market, check with your paint dealer. Tell him what your problem is. If it is, say, abnormal mildew growth, you can buy a paint containing a mildewcide. Do you live in a highly industrial locality? Most good-quality paints on the market are at least somewhat resistant to industrial fumes, but there are in addition paints that are especially fume-resistant.

WOOD COATINGS

Color Selection

Selecting colors is perhaps the most enjoyable aspect of a paint job, but care should be taken. It may be several years before an interior needs repainting and more than that for an exterior—if you make a mistake, you will have a long time to learn to dislike the color.

Your main color considerations, no doubt, will be that the colors are, by themselves, good-looking and that they will combine harmoniously with each other.

You can explore entire books on color selection, but they tend to be contradictory and confusing. Far better is to visualize colors in action—in your rooms, on your house—and choose what you like.

◄ With only this room as evidence, it would not be hard to guess the favorite color of the interior designer who planned the scheme. Yet only a few years ago he would have been regarded as a heretic for using purple in such profusion. That is the way decorating fashions are: changeable. Rely on your instincts. If someone says, "That color is out this year," tell him to wait until *next* year.

That certain colors arouse similar emotions in us is proved by the picture above. It does not remind you of an ice-blue, sub-zero day in Antarctica, does it? More likely an early-summer's day in the Southwest. Note, too, how the yellows and reds draw us into the setting, make things seem closer. If cool colors had been used here, the objects would seem to recede from us.

Color inspirations

Color ideas can come from many sources. You might glean them from the homes of friends, neighbors, or acquaintances. Another good source is publications. Books and, especially, magazines teem with color photographs. Then it is a matter of mentally transplanting the colors to your own home. It might be even simpler than that. It is not unusual for someone to admire a color in another person's home and to learn, by asking directly, the specific paint brand and tint and the store where it was bought.

Just remember that the colors in publications and other people's houses will not look exactly the same in your house. Photographs do not reproduce colors truly. The condition—mainly the porosity—of surfaces in your home can make even identical brands of paint look slightly darker or lighter.

Also, while we are loath to lay down any rules about color, do not forget that what you select should harmonize with the accessories inside your home or outside—flowers, grass, trees, and so on.

Fool the eye with colors

Color can do more for your home than make it good-looking. It has other important functions. One, apparently, is to change the architecture visually.

For example, if you have a huge room or house, you can make it appear smaller by painting it a dark color, such as brown or olive green.

Conversely, if you want to make a small area look larger, choose a light color—cream, beige, yellow, and so on. Compare two side-by-side houses, the smaller one white and the other

gray, and you would swear that the white one is bigger. And you would be wrong.

Dark and light colors can be combined for fool-the-eye architectural effects. For instance, if you have a room shaped like a bowling alley and would like it to seem wider, use a dark color on the short end walls and a lighter color on the long side walls.

Color can unify. If your house is constructed of several materials, painting it two shades of the same color will bring the elements together. Or, if you have added dormers, let them pick up the major color of the siding, and you will minimize the sore-thumb effect that is so often the result of this home improvement.

Use color for atmosphere

Color can establish the mood of a setting. Warm colors—reds and yellows—tend to make us feel cozy and cheerful, while cool colors—blues and greens—are neutral and relaxing. Many people have an inclination, also, to think of blues and greens as institutional colors suitable only for hospitals and offices. This is chiefly a result, however, of faulty color sense and lack of imagination; soft tones and slightly offbeat tints are most attractive in domestic interiors.

Add lightness with color

Yet another use of color is to brighten rooms. Rule: the lighter the color, the more light it reflects and the brighter the area it covers. Vivid yellow might be just the thing for that bedroom with one small window in the back of the house. It is not happenstance that many basements are painted white.

You should select wall colors with some reference to the light and the view the room commands—a room overlooking a lake, say, might well be painted blue. It is a common decorating mistake to try to subdue the brightness of a west-facing room by painting its walls blue. In fact, blue will look namby-pamby in the brilliant afternoon sun, while the same sun will enliven yellows and oranges.

A revised color scheme was an essential part of the remodeling job done on this dining room. The job included the installation of French doors, replacement of windows, and the removal of a tiled floor and refinishing of the original oak floor. The new color scheme features warm hues massed in a grouping that gives the room focus and direction. The neutrals selected temper the bright colors, preventing them from dominating.

Tips on Buying Paints

To get the maximum value from your painting dollar, you should know a few things before visiting the paint store. Here is a grab bag of hints on costs and pitfalls that can be avoided.

The first area to be covered when you paint a room is the ceiling. Beginning at one corner, paint a narrow strip across the room's shallower dimension. If possible, paint toward a window; the light reflecting off the wet paint helps you to keep your strokes even and helps to show where you have already painted. Keep strips narrow so that you can start a new one before the first has dried; wet paint applied over dry will leave lap marks.

When painting a wall, you should start at an upper corner, painting a strip several feet long at the ceiling line. Moving downward and in a roughly diagonal direction, gradually fill in the large triangular area between the end of the strip and the lower corner of the wall. This method will assure you of the "wet edge."

When you paint around doors and windows, make your first strokes perpendicular to the trim, cutting in with the edge of the brush as close as possible and painting away from the trim. The last stroke, made with the edge of the brush, is made parallel with the woodwork. End the stroke by lifting the brush away from trim.

■ Buy only as much paint as you will need, but do not underestimate the amount—the extra quarts you buy piecemeal will be appreciably more expensive than paint bought by the gallon. And you may have trouble matching color if you have used an unusual mix. If you tell your paint dealer the square footage of the area to be painted, he can advise on the quantity of paint needed.

■ If you want a light, common color such as pale pink for an interior wall that requires no great subtlety of coloration, you can buy white paint and a tube of colorant and mix your own. It is not difficult (you just add colorant to the white and mix away), and it is the least expensive way to buy paint. Tell or show your dealer the color you have in mind, and he will give you the appropriate colorant. If you will need many gallons of the color, buy the colorant by the can—it is cheaper than by the tube. But be sure to mix all the paint at one time; your chances of hitting the same proportions a second time are nonexistent.

■ If you do want a definite or unusual color, look at many manufacturers' ready-mix color-chip cards before asking the dealer to custom-mix the paint. Different manufacturers have different ideas of what supposedly constitutes the same color—and this results in many versions of even standard colors like ivory, which may vary greatly in both hue and tone. So you may be able to find a ready-mix and not have to spend extra for custom-mixing.

■ If you need benzene or turpentine, ask your dealer whether he sells it in bulk. Some dealers keep on hand large supplies of these solvents and will fill any metal container you bring— much less expensive than the packaged kind.

■ Do not buy "odorless" thinner. It is not cheap, and in any event, although the thinner may not smell, the paint will.

■ Buy all the paint you need from one dealer at one time. He will give you, free, painting hats, sticks, and advice—and may even deliver the paint.

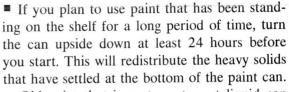

Hints on Using Paint

Every trade has its tricks, and painting is no exception to the rule. Below and in the photographs are some basic techniques for working with paint.

■ Ask your dealer to give you fresh paint. The fresher it is, the easier it is to mix.

■ If you plan to use paint that has been standing on the shelf for a long period of time, turn the can upside down at least 24 hours before you start. This will redistribute the heavy solids that have settled at the bottom of the paint can.

■ Old paint that is part crust, part liquid can be strained through a piece of screen. The resultant mixture can be used as a prime coat, but will be unsatisfactory for finish coats.

If you intend to store paint for a few days or longer, the can lids should be tapped securely in place with a hammer to seal the paint against air. Annoyingly, though, paint does collect in can rims, and when you tap the lids, paint can spatter you—or perhaps worse, that freshly painted nearby wall. To avoid this, drape a cloth over the lid, as shown at left; then proceed with the hammer. Now spatters go only into the cloth.

While paint that runs down a can onto dropcloths or newspapers will not get on the protected floor, it can be carried to an unprotected one: you step on drippings and unwittingly track them about. One trick to prevent this is to wipe paint off can occasionally with your brush. Another is shown at left: glue paper plate, rim up, to bottom of can. Paint runs harmlessly onto it. To be doubly safe, lay newspaper paths wherever you walk.

If you are going to store paint only overnight, you need not go to the trouble of tightly sealing each can. Just dribble on the paint a little of the thinner you are using; then press the lid loosely in place. The thinner will float on the paint, like cream on milk, and air cannot penetrate. The next day, when you are ready to resume painting, stir in the film of thinner. If you are using a canned thinner, hold the can with its spout located as shown: this keeps liquid from slopping down the container's side.

All paints except the most specialized require thorough mixing before use. Best way to accomplish this is by "boxing"—pouring back and forth between two cans. After opening a fresh can, pour about a third of the paint into another can. Stir paint left in first can, using a figure-8 (not a round-and-round) motion. When it is smooth, pour it into the second can. Then proceed to box until all the paint is the same consistency. If thinner is needed, add it to first can after pouring off top third.

Punching holes in the can rim is a good way to minimize amount of paint that invariably collects there. Holes let paint run back into can. Make a dozen or so holes, evenly spaced, with a hammer and a nail. Do not use an electric drill. A spark could ignite paint fumes.

Petroleum jelly is helpful when you are painting. Spread a very thin film of it on exposed skin before you start. Paint spatters will wipe away easily after the job. Also, use jelly to remove dried paint from skin. Apply it to affected area; wait five minutes; then wipe off.

Preparation for Painting

To do a good paint job, you must prepare properly—get the old surface ready for the new paint. The better you prepare, the better the paint will look.

Exterior preparation

The most common outside task you are likely to have is removing blistered or peeling paint. It all must go, down to clean, bare wood if possible, or at least to sound, well-adhering paint.

For small areas, a scraper—it looks like a spatula—is the best tool, although a putty knife will do. If a good deal of paint must be removed, you can buy a special hooked scraper that looks like a back-scratcher—except that, instead of scratchers, it has a tough blade. This tool has lots of leverage and takes off paint quickly and well. A wire brush is good for following up after you have gotten rid of most of the paint and for removing paint that is peeling.

When you have scraped away all the loose paint possible, use a medium-grit sandpaper to smooth the edges of the sound paint around scraped areas. Then spot-prime them (apply a light coat of your finish paint). The purpose is to bring these areas level with the surrounding paint, so that they will be invisible later, and to prevent bare wood from bleeding (showing) through the new paint.

If you discover that the old paint is peeling to bare wood, rather than just to the next layer of paint, you probably have moisture trouble. Moisture has worked its way behind the paint film and is pushing it off. Reducing the amount of water vapor generated inside the house—by such things as washing machine and showers—should help solve this problem.

Caulking is the material that seals all the joints—seams, you might say—in a house: between door and window frames and walls, house corners, and so on. If caulking is cracked or missing, replace it. For a job that will really last

—10 or more years—use one of the new sealers instead of caulking. Your paint dealer can tell you all about the types available.

Also, check window putty. Replace as necessary with putty or one of the new sealers.

Usually, you do not have to clean the house exterior unless dirt accumulations are heavy. If they are, use trisodium phosphate (Soilax), and rinse well.

Proper preparation includes making all carpentry-type repairs: tap in loose nails; repair broken siding; readjust gutter pitch so water cannot overflow onto the siding. The main idea is to keep water out of the walls. Doing this eliminates almost all potential problems you can have with paint.

Interior preparation

First, clean off heavy dirt, all wax, and all grease. Remove all switch plates, light fixtures, and picture hooks, and repair any holes in the plaster or dry wall. Then dust the walls, paying particular attention to moldings.

Having the proper tools will make preparing your home for painting very much easier. Useful outside tools are: scraper, hooked scraper (for removing peeling paint from large areas), putty knife, wire brush, hammer (for renailing loose siding), old brush (for dusting), screwdriver (for removing caulking), caulking gun, and medium-grit sandpaper. Scraper, dust brush, putty knife, and steel wool are useful for preparing interior walls and ceilings.

Window screens, screen doors, storm windows, and shutters should be taken down and given a careful dusting. An old paintbrush is ideal for this, although any soft-bristled brush will do. Paint these items while they are down: reattach them after the house has been painted.

Besides dusting screens and shutters, you should dust the house. You need not do everything, only areas where dirt has accumulated, such as under window sills and eaves. It is a good idea, though, to carry the dust brush while you are painting, so you can dust as needed.

Scraper with an angled blade 3½ inches wide is helpful for both interior and exterior preparation. While it can be used to remove peeling paint indoors and out, it is *the* tool for making plaster patches. Buy one with a flexible blade —brace the blade with your forefinger.

After you get off most of the peeling paint with a scraper, follow with a wire brush. This will dispose of fine particles the scraper cannot handle. Next, sand with medium-grit sandpaper. Then spot-prime the scraped areas. Peeling paint reveals that siding has a serious moisture problem.

Handiest tool for caulking is a caulking gun. You slip in a cartridge of caulking, squeeze the trigger, and the caulking emerges in a neat, thin bead. Keep the pressure on the trigger steady. If you need only a little caulking, you can buy it in a can and apply it with a putty knife, spoon handle, or your finger; or in a tube, which has a nozzle applicator.

Use putty knife to dig out dried and cracked putty. Work the knife tip between putty and window frame, and pry up. Putty will come out in big chunks. Follow by scraping wood with knife edge to clear away all adhering pieces; then dust off all loose matter. Fresh putty or other sealer will not adhere to a surface that is not absolutely clean.

Before applying new glazing compound, brush dust and loose material off wood and glass. The portion of the glass to be covered with compound should be painted to assure a good bond and waterproof seal. For a smooth surface, run a dusting brush over the compound before it has set.

Check nails in siding, and replace any that are not firm. Use a nail set and hammer to sink heads below the surface, then fill holes with caulking or glazing compound, removing any excess with the tip of a putty knife. If nailheads are flush, prime each of them with a dab of paint.

With today's paints, you can leave some rust on metal, but not *loose* rust. Prepare surface by getting rid of all loose rust with a wire brush or electric drill with grinding attachment; then coat with rust-inhibiting primer. Follow with a coat of rust-resistant finish paint or, really, any kind of paint you wish.

If walls and ceilings are plaster, they probably have some cracks or holes. These should be filled with spackling compound and then made flush with surrounding surfaces.

Dig out all unsound plaster from cracks with a scraper, beer-can opener with hooked end, or screwdriver. Clear away crumbly material with a stiff brush.

Douse the cleaned cracks with water; then fill them with a buttery (not loose) mixture of patching plaster and water. Smooth this with vertical passes (up and down along the crack) with your scraper held almost flat against the wall. The key to smoothness is using a scraper with a flexible blade. You should sand to remove minor imperfections. But do not depend on sanding to dispose of a bumpy patch; this is very difficult to do.

Holes require two applications of plaster: wet hole, fill halfway with plaster, let dry, wet down, apply more plaster.

If no backup material, like lath (thin wood strips), shows in a hole, fill it with soaked newspaper or steel wool. Then proceed with the two coats of plaster.

When you fix any patch, wait until it is completely dry; then spot-prime it. Let this dry completely, too. Now patch is ready for the painting.

Dry-wall construction usually does not develop cracks or holes. But nails do come loose. Tap these slightly below the surface and fill the dimple depressions with joint cement. (This is sold at hardware stores.)

How to paint trim

A 2½- or 3-inch brush is usually preferred for painting interior and exterior trim, but choose a smaller brush if that suits you. You will merely go a little slower.

In preparing trim for painting, be sure that surfaces are clean and dry. If you are applying enamel over enamel, fine; if enamel over flat, all right; but if you are putting flat over enamel, first sand off the gloss for good adhesion. If you get fresh paint on a previously painted surface, just wipe it off with a rag dampened in the solvent.

Exterior Painting

You will no doubt find the actual painting of your house much more satisfying than the preparation. It is a fine feeling, after all that scrubbing, sanding, scraping, and caulking, to watch the house take on bright new life as the paint flows from your brush. All your effort becomes worthwhile.

To minimize problems and make the job as good and easy as possible, there are some tips and techniques you should be mindful of.

First, cover up adequately. This means that bushes, shrubbery, concrete, blacktop, stone walks, and the like should be protected against

Key to neat painting of window is angle at which you hold brush. Angle above—about 45 degrees—is correct. This lets you rest more bristles on the wood, which steadies the brush, and more of wood's surface is visible. Paint all parts of the window, even awkward ones, from 45-degree angle. Proper positioning of ladder makes this easier.

Woodwork should be prepared as carefully as the rest of the house. Fill holes with putty, clear away dust, and wash off heavy accumulations of soil with trisodium phosphate, being sure to rinse well. Also, scrape off peeling paint, and sand scraped areas thoroughly. Good trick for working with sandpaper is to wrap it around block of wood.

Woodwork should be painted going, as the professionals say, from the dry into the wet. Place paint-filled brush on dry area about a foot ahead of previously painted section; then brush back until you overlap. Finish with long, smooth strokes, holding the brush lightly but firmly. Brushing too hard may result in unsightly brush marks.

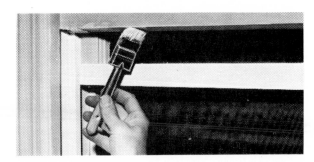

To save time and not miss any areas, paint a window in definite sequence. Raise bottom sash until it is about a foot from top of opening; pull top sash down until a little more than half of it is accessible. Paint all exposed parts of both sashes and of pulley channels. Adjust sashes so you can paint rest of top one and channels. Paint framing.

Best way to paint baseboards is to "dry-brush" them. Dip the brush about halfway into the paint, and paint a strip of baseboard about 3 feet long and as deep as three-quarters of the baseboard's width. After you do this, brush will be almost dry, and you can use its remaining paint to cut in near the floor.

paint spatters—there are bound to be some. Best covers you can buy are canvas dropcloths. Good ones are made of heavy fabric that paint cannot penetrate (it will seep through cheap ones) and will last for years. Three 8x12-foot cloths should be sufficient.

If you would rather not invest in these, you can use old sheets or the cheap 8x12-foot plastic dropcloths sold at paint stores. But, unlike canvas cloths, they must be tied around bushes so they will not blow off. Walkways can be covered with overlapping sheets of newspaper.

Masonry that is part of the house structure and door and window screens, unless you take them down (which is advisable), also should be protected. Spatters on these materials are really troublesome. All you can do is try to take them off with the thinner you are using. But you will leave cloudy blotches where you have cleaned. Dried paint on masonry is even worse. It is removed—or you attempt removal—with a difficult liquid called muriatic acid.

Best and easiest protection is newspapers affixed with masking tape. You need not cover the entire exposed surface—just the top few feet below where you are painting. Paint drops have a way of not falling straight down. A trick with masking tape: pretape the newspaper—half the sticky part on the paper, half off—before attaching it.

Cover yourself, too. Wear pants, a hat, and, even if the weather is hot, a long-sleeved shirt; you should expose as little skin as possible. Greatest thing for cleaning paint off skin is a pretty pink lanolin-base cream (buy it at paint stores) that looks as if it could not clean anything. But it is sensational. You dab it on, wait a minute, then wipe off the paint like magic. And it leaves your skin smooth.

Also, wear stiff-soled shoes. They are best for ladder climbing.

Painting with a ladder

Even professional house-painters must use ladders—scaffolding is impractical in terms of both time and money. But keep in mind that an apalling proportion of our national accident rate is attributable to ladders. Make sure your ladder is a good one and in good repair. If you do not

own a ladder, you can rent one. For easier handling, choose an aluminum one; it weighs only half as much as a wooden one—a fact you will appreciate as the painting progresses.

Use the ladder safely. (1) When you lean it against a wall, the distance between ladder bottom and wall base should be no more than a third the ladder's total length. So a 16-foot ladder should not be much more than 5 feet from the wall. (2) Do not let the legs stand on soft ground. Set them on a board. (3) Do not use a ladder when one of its legs is higher than the other. Clamp a stout board on the short leg to make the legs even.

Unless you rent expensive scaffolding, you will have to reach the high points of your house with a standard rung-type ladder. However, for painting the lower portions, you can rent cheaply a couple of brackets called ladder jacks, which are great. You lean two ladders, or two halves of a ladder, against the house and attach a jack to each. Then you lay a couple of planks from jack to jack, and you have an instant scaffold. You can paint more from one positioning of the ladders, and the work is easier and faster than with a single ladder.

Whatever kind of paint you use, follow the manufacturer's instructions to the letter. If mix-

◄ Though large, the Cape Cod-style home, left, was not difficult to paint. Shutters were taken down and painted separately. Most of the clapboard siding and trim is so low that it could be painted from a stepladder. Even getting to high spots with an extension ladder was fairly simple, because there are no architectural obstructions to interfere with ladder placement.

Those with fear of heights would appreciate this house, above. A 10- or 12-foot rung ladder and a stepladder would be tall enough to reach every section. If you are dismayed by high places, you can still paint your house— at least half of it. You do the lower part and arrange for a professional to do the upper. Many painters will agree to this—and will probably give you some helpful advice.

ing or stirring is prescribed, and it almost always is, you can mix more paint at one time more easily with 2-gallon buckets. It is also easier to work with a big-mouth 2-gallon can, and no time is wasted snaking your brush through a narrow mouth into the paint. Order paint in as many 2-gallon buckets as possible. If you need 11 gallons, get 10 of them in 2-gallon form.

Brushes are best for both siding and exterior trim (windows, eaves, gutters, etc.). Rollers are not recommended, except for masonry, block walls, and similar rough surfaces, where a long-nap roller does well.

As a general rule, avoid painting in the sun. Although some paints are unaffected by sunlight, the heat may cause others to wrinkle or blister as they dry. This may, of course, mean that painting the front of the house is a morning job, while finishing the back of the house is an afternoon job.

If your house is so situated that you cannot avoid painting in sunshine, do so early in the morning before the sun is hot. Chances are that nothing will happen to the paint. But why look for trouble when you can avoid it?

Also, do not paint when the weather is too hot or too cold, say above 90 or below 40 degrees. See the can label for exact temperatures.

Painting sections of your house in a planned sequence will reduce the number of times you must reposition the ladder. There are also ways to paint from a ladder to achieve maximum coverage while you are up there.

Whenever possible, paint areas directly above the ladder. Start at the top of the siding, and work your way across it, covering sections about three or four courses deep and four or five feet wide. When you get to the end of the siding, you will have a horizontal band of paint right across the house. Then paint another horizontal band below this one, and so on. Remember, when you get to the lower parts, you can use the ladder jack arrangement mentioned above.

If you are fast with a brush—and a little ambidextrous—you can paint from one ladder position not only the area above the ladder, but those on both sides of it as far down as you can reach. The paint will look like an upside-down U. Then move the ladder below the U, and fill in the empty place. This is the way the professionals do it. The method does, however, require speed of execution. If you do not work fast enough, the already applied paint—especially latex—will partially dry, and the places where you overlap will show.

Paint the undermost edge of weatherboarding first, being sure that cracks are filled with paint. Then paint the face of the board. Do not overload your brush. An excess of paint on the surface is difficult to work with, and the paint has an unfortunate tendency to "load" in the heel of the brush. Only the lower third of the bristles should be dipped in the paint.

Use the tip of the brush to work paint into crevices around window and door frames and corner boards. Paint should seal the cracks. Hold the brush lightly but firmly, as shown here, with the fingers draped over the ferrule. The flagged ends of the bristles, not their sides, should do the work. When you paint the face of the boards, move the brush in steady strokes parallel with the edges.

Applying paint

Above all, do not be afraid to use paint. Most inexperienced painters sin on the side of stinginess. They stroke on a brushful, but then scrub it out to cover a larger area than it is supposed to.

There is no way to explain precisely how much paint to use. Generally, though, if you keep dipping your brush about halfway into the paint, then gently tapping on the inside of the can, then applying it, and dipping again just before the brush starts to pull, you will be using enough. The idea is to let the paint do the work, lubricating the way for the brush. If you follow this technique, you should be able to cover from 450 to 550 square feet of siding with a gallon of paint. In rare cases, manufacturers recommend heavier coverage. Check the label.

While the above may tell you how much paint to use, it does not say how to apply it. This varies, depending on the siding.

If you are painting something smooth, like clapboard, first cut in the bottom of the boards; then paint the face of each. Paint from the dry into the wet: start a foot or so away from the already-applied paint, and brush back into the wet area, making your final strokes long and light to smooth it all.

This dry-into-wet method also is recommended for relatively smooth material like asbestos shingles; but make your finishing strokes up and down, following the grooves.

Deeply grooved siding, such as machine-cut shakes, cannot be painted horizontally. Instead, jam the end of the brush between courses; then apply the paint with a wiping motion, following the grooves (or striations, as they are also called). Using a good brush on shakes will effectively ruin it. Use an old, worn-down brush. It will do a fine job, and you will not sacrifice a good brush. If you do not own an old one, a worthwhile investment is a brush, relatively new on the market, that looks like a scrub brush with a handle. It has short, tough bristles, one row

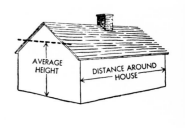

Multiply the distance in feet around house by its average height plus 2 feet, to get square feet of surface to be painted. One gallon of finish covers about 500 square feet, but check label on can of paint.

of which is separated from the others for cutting in between courses. You wipe on the paint as you would if using a scrub brush.

Trim (woodwork), of course, calls for a good brush. Here again, use the dry-into-wet method.

As you paint, keep an eye out for drippings onto the siding or woodwork. Wipe them off immediately, while they are wet. Also make touch-ups, if necessary, while the paint is wet.

Problems

Painting problems most often have to do with paint already on a surface, although they are not limited to this. A number of them are defined below, accompanied by suggested solutions.

■ Alligatoring: So called because the paint—it can be inside or outside the house—has cracked apart into little segments and resembles an alligator's skin. This may result from a variety of causes, including the perennial bugaboo, moisture, but most commonly it is due to paint incompatibility. It is usually seen where flat paint has been applied over enamel—on doors and other woodwork. The flat paint could not get a holding grip on the nonporous enamel.

The most effective way to treat an alligatored surface is to remove all the paint, then apply compatible primer and finish coat. Paint can be removed chemically with any of several paint removers, or by heat (a blowtorch or a special high-temperature, flameless heating unit). In frankness, neither of these remedies is recommended to the do-it-yourselfer. A safer, but much more laborious method, is to clean the wood with a power sander.

Before you decide on any of these drastic steps, try this: prepare a slurry of spackle (normally used to fill cracks and holes in plastered surfaces)—that is, a loose, wet mixture. Smear it all over the affected door or woodwork, filling the depressions and smoothing the spackle even with the islands of paint. Let dry completely (4 to 5 hours or longer). Then paint with a primer compatible with the paint already on the door. Let this dry thoroughly, then apply your finish coat of paint.

■ Fading: Here, the paint just fades, the way color comes out of a dress during repeated washings. The cause: the paint is of poor quality. Solution: use good-quality paint.

■ Crawling: So named because freshly applied paint contracted into puddles and droplets like water on a greased frying pan. Crawling can be caused by not having removed grease and grime before painting or by having painted in cold or humid weather. The cure is prevention: clean surface thoroughly; paint only in weather specified by the manufacturer on the paint-can label.

■ Bleeding: This refers to plaster patches that show through the finish coat and to exudation of discoloring oils by certain woods. Western red cedar is an example.

In the first instance, bleeding can occur because: (1) finish coat was applied over a patch without the patch being primed; (2) patch was primed, but finish coat was put on before primer had dried completely; (3) primer was applied while patch was wet; (4) patch painted with enamel was not primed with shellac. The solution to all four is, of course, to go back and do the job that should have been done in the first place.

Another kind of bleeding is caused by the exudation of pitch or resin around knots in the lower grades of lumber, especially pine. The affected area must be cleaned and treated with knot sealer, then repainted. If there is a pocket of pitch located below the surface, drill a hole, allow the pitch to drain, then putty the hole, seal it, and repaint. Isolated stains caused by

The first step in painting the exterior is to cut in on the underside of overlapped boards, being sure to work paint well into all corners and cracks. The job can be done with either a brush or a small, specially designed roller.

Cover shrubbery, walks, and flower beds with drop cloths to avoid splattering paint on them. Trees and overhanging branches can be tied out of the way, and the drop cloth secured with a short length of stout rope.

When painting with brush, use the flat of the tip in long, level strokes for a smooth surface. At bottom of siding, as here, point tip downward in order to avoid accidentally smearing paint on the masonry foundation.

Wide rollers, designed for use on flat exterior surfaces, assure the amateur painter a fast, smooth application of paint. Be sure to run the roller over surface several times so that paint will work into cracks.

Moisture did this—rather, water. It sneaked into house where caulking was missing, seeped into walls, and emerged through paint. Check all possible entries. Only by finding source can problem be corrected. Unfortunately, all paint must be removed.

Moisture did this, too. It got into wood through open joints in window framing. If joints had been puttied, this would not have happened. The only solution is to remove all paint down to bare wood. A small propane torch will do that well enough.

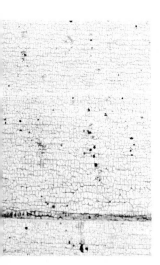

Siding here has paint that is checking—separating with fine criss-crossing hairline cracks. The trouble can usually be traced to insufficient drying time between coats of paint. Sand checked paint smooth with No. 1 sandpaper; spot-prime.

These are temperature blisters, caused by painting in the sun. They differ from moisture blisters, which have water in them. Cure: wait a week; scrape off all peeling and blistered paint to sound paint; sand edges of scraped areas; then spot-prime .

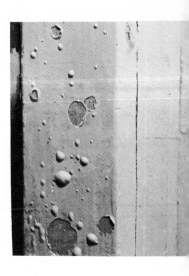

Resin bleeding is an unsightly condition resulting from painting over unsealed knots and pitch pockets. Bleeding can be prevented by using properly cured dry wood, and sealing all knots and pitch areas. In extreme cases, aluminum powder can be added to the sealer. Allow the sealer to dry at least two hours before beginning to paint.

Alligatoring is caused by the uneven expansion and contraction of a top coat over a slippery primer coat. The condition may result from applying enamel over an oil primer, painting over a greasy surface, painting over asphalt, pitch, shellac, or bituminous paint, or not allowing sufficient drying time between coats.

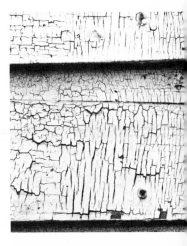

Paint on metal downspouts should be smoothed with downward strokes of the brush. Do not let paint build up in corrugations at the elbow. If you have replaced old downspouts, new galvanized metal should be allowed to weather for six months before you apply metal primer.

Before you begin to paint, remove hardware like house numbers. If the light fixture is irremovable, hold it away from the wall with one hand as you paint under it with the other. Screw the fixture back in place while paint is wet so that a seal will form around the collar.

minor bleeding can be scraped and washed with mineral spirits, providing the paint has not been damaged.

■ Loss of gloss and color: This happens when paint was brushed on too thinly or when too much thinner (thinning agent) was used. Woodwork with this problem has less color in some places, or less gloss, or both. Solution: when repainting, follow manufacturer's label directions for mixing, and to forestall a recurrence, do not be stingy with paint.

■ Chalking: Many good-quality paints are designed to chalk gradually. Color washes off them, taking dirt with it. But if the paint is of poor quality, chalking is acute and rapid. Solution: prime with an *oil-base* paint before refinishing with the paint you like. Also, do not use any kind of chalking paint above brick or other colored masonry which will show streaks as the chalk washes down the wall.

■ Flaking: Paint falls off like autumn leaves. This is especially common with galvanized metal. Solution for new galvanized metal: let it weather six months before painting it. For old: remove loose paint. Consult your dealer to learn which paints will offer the best adhesion to metal surfaces.

■ Wrinkling: Symptom: paint looks wrinkled. Causes: too-heavy application of paint; applying paint in the sun. Cure: sand off wrinkles; repaint according to label directions.

■ Mildew: This is one of the painting problems most frequently encountered, at least outside the dry Western states. Mildew, a fungus, grows on painted surfaces and does an effective job of discoloring them.

One trouble with mildew is that it looks like ordinary soil, so people treat it as such—and never succeed in getting it all off.

Actually, you can detect differences. Mildew has a more grayish, cobweblike appearance than does dirt. To make sure, daub some bleach on the discolored patches. If the stain disappears, it is probably mildew; if it remains, it is dirt.

To remove mildew, scrub with a solution of $\frac{2}{3}$ cup trisodium phosphate (for example, Soilax), $\frac{1}{3}$ cup detergent, 1 quart household bleach to 3 quarts warm water. Wear rubber gloves while you scrub. Repeated washings may be required.

Average paint coverage, brush painting

	Approximate number of square feet covered by one gallon		
	*Used as one coat	*Used as two coats	*Used as three coats
Exterior house paint			
Wood siding	. .470. .	. .250. .	. .180. .
Shingle siding	. .340. .	. .190. .	
Exterior trim paint, wood trim	. .850. .	. .435. .	. .300. .
Exterior oil paint			
Brick	. .200. .	. .150. .	
Cement, cinder block	. .180. .	. .105. .	
Stucco	. .150. .	. .125. .	. .100. .
Exterior cement water paint			
Brick	. .100. .	. .60. .	
Cement, cinder block	. .100. .	. .60. .	
Stucco	. .100. .	. .60. .	
Shingle stain			
Shingle siding	. .150. .	. .90. .	
Shingle roof	. .120. .	. .80. .	
Porch and deck paint			
Wood	. .380. .	. .200. .	. .165. .
Concrete	. .450. .	. .260. .	. .180. .
Flat oil paint, plaster (over primer)	. .540. .	. .290. .	
Gloss oil paint, plaster (over primer)	. .540. .	. .270. .	
Emulsion paint or casein-water paint, plaster	. .540. .	. .310. .	
Enamel, interior trim (over primer)	. .400. .	. .225. .	
Varnish, floor	. .540. .	. .270. .	. .180. .
Shellac, floor	. .540. .	. .300. .	. .220. .

*Example: One gallon of exterior oil paint, properly applied, will cover approximately 200 square feet of unpainted brick with one coat. The first coat efficiently seals the porous brick, however, so that considerably less paint is required for the second coat. Thus the same gallon of oil paint will be sufficient to cover 150 square feet of brick with two coats.

Interior Painting

The first step in painting a room is to move out all the furniture or group it at room center. Before you cover it, stand on your ladder to see if you can reach the middle of the ceiling, above the furniture, with your roller. This is usually the least accessible place. If you can reach it, you should be able to reach the rest of the ceiling. Then make sure there is enough space between walls and furniture for you to paint walls without difficulty. You want to avoid moving furniture once you have started painting. That not only wastes time but involves a different kind of energy, and you might find it exhausting.

Cover the furniture with canvas dropcloths or cheap plastic dropcloths held down by old sheets so the light plastic will not slip or drift away. Floors can be covered with canvas dropcloths or overlapping pieces of newspaper. As mentioned before, make newspaper paths into other rooms you may go to during the job. Shoes can pick up paint drippings on coverings and track them into unprotected areas.

Using flat paint
Most people prefer flat paint in living rooms, bedrooms, hallways—everywhere except the kitchen and bathroom, where enamel is the choice. Reason: flat has low light reflectance, so it is easier on the eyes, more restful. Too, it is mostly roller applied.

When you paint interiors, it is advisable to take on only one room at a time. It is also best to establish and follow a definite sequence of steps. For a one-coat job, do the ceiling first: wash away heavy dirt, and patch as necessary. While these patches are drying (about 10 minutes if you use plaster of paris), clean and patch the walls. Then prime the ceiling patches with a light coat of your finish paint; now prime the wall patches. By the time you finish these, the ceiling primes should be dry, and you can

With modern fast-drying paints, the dining room at right could well be painted in a single day, despite its two-tone color scheme. Dark red flat paint is almost certainly a one-coat job, although the lighter wall might require two coats for complete coverage. The cream-colored baseboard gives sharp definition to the junction of the varnished parquet floor and the dark red wall, but demands a firm painting hand to ensure a clean line.

start painting. When you have completed the ceiling, the wall patches will be dry, and you can paint the walls. In this way, you never have to wait for anything to dry—and patches and primes must be allowed to dry thoroughly before succeeding steps are taken—and can work steadily without interruption.

For a two-coat job, the procedure is different. Prepare the walls first; do the ceiling patches; then prime the wall patches. While these are drying, prime the ceiling patches. Probably by the time you have primed the last patch the first one will be dry, especially if you are using latex flat paint. Then give the ceiling both coats; with modern fast-drying paints, you can probably apply both on the same day. And finally, paint the walls.

The primer used on walls, by the way, can also be an extra-thin coat of your finish paint.

Remember that most rooms do not need two coats of paint, unless you are changing from a dark to a light color or you have made an abnormal number of patches. If you are going from a light color to a darker one, a single coat will suffice.

Because it serves as part of a fluorescent lighting system and reflects very brilliant light, white ceiling shown above is bound to attract attention. Painting must be precise, preparation of the surface meticulous.

A big piece of furniture is a candidate for painting with flat, but you should follow with a clear finish for protection against soil and wear. Storage unit in this room was given this treatment, with moldings accented in gold. Paint stores sell small bottles of metallic paint.

Living room at right presents a hazard ▶ that most people fear: getting paint on ceiling when cutting in a flush (no molding) wall. You need not worry. Cut in with *bold* strokes (boldness yields a straighter line). If you do overlap paint on the ceiling, wipe it away. Even if you left it, nobody would notice it unless he stood right beside the wall and looked straight up.

Painting with enamel

For washability, nothing beats enamel. And this single factor makes it ideal for kitchens, baths, woodwork, and other areas subject to excessive soil and wear.

Enamels are available in both oil-base (solvent-thinned) and latex (water-thinned) form. The former comes in high gloss and semigloss, the latter in semigloss only. Although latex enamels have developed considerably since their introduction a few years ago, they are still not quite the equal in covering power of their oil-base counterparts. Nevertheless, they can do the job, especially if you are using a color darker than the one already on the surface. And, of course, they do have the tremendous advantage of being water soluble.

Prepare surfaces to be painted with enamel as you would any others, except prime the plaster patches with shellac (3-pound cut) instead of paint. You need not wash the entire surface, but do remove heavy accumulations of soil and all grease. Trisodium phosphate and warm water will do this.

It is best to apply enamel with a brush. Paint areas about 3 feet square. Put on the paint with swirling, any-direction strokes, concentrating on covering the maximum dry area with each stroke. Then make all your finishing strokes in one direction.

In a typical kitchen, do the closets and cupboards first, working from the inside out, the ceiling next, then the walls, and, finally, the windows. Follow this routine for a bathroom. Woodwork to be enameled should be painted after the walls have dried.

When you paint pipes, turn the heat off temporarily and paint the pipes the same color as the walls or ceiling. As a general rule, you should not use aluminum paint on pipes—it

As cool as the filtered green light on the forest floor, this serenely elegant dining room takes its color scheme from the gold and apple green of the panes in a nineteenth-century stained-glass window. Antique chairs and accessories are painted a glossy green.

◄Louvered closet doors, across page, where fingerprints might be expected, were finished with glossy enamel for easy cleaning. The enamel was carefully mixed to match the yellow matte paint on bedroom walls.

will make them stand out like sore thumbs. The rule can, of course, be broken; if you are painting a chilly basement workroom, you may want to take the reflective heat and let the aesthetics go hang.

Finishes

While floor finishes are not usually paint jobs, except on decks and in basements, the properties of varnish and other finish materials have much in common with paint. As with painting, the preparation of the surface is half the battle and needs careful attention.

Today a great variety of floor finishes is available, some better for do-it-yourself use than others. All, however, require presanding—if you want that wonder-working effect. To presand, you need a large, drum-type sander and some skill. If you are not especially handy, you had better have it done professionally. But if you would like to give it a whirl, you can rent a sander from a paint dealer or a store that specializes in tool rental. Full instructions on use come with it. (It is advisable, by the way, to refinish your floors before you paint your walls—the sanding process kicks up a lot of dust.)

Proper preparation of the surface may require filling in deep scratches with wood-paste filler or wood plastic. For accurate and unobtrusive results, apply the filler with a small brush and sand it flush with the floor.

Of the many types of finish, four seem particularly suited to do-it-yourself application.

■ Shellac: A most versatile finish (see photographs), shellac is the old standby, the most popular clear coating, favored by many people because it is so easy to apply and dries so quickly that a two- or three-coat job is possible in a day. It is durable, but can cloud up if water or alcohol is spilled on it. To protect against spills, wax the floor after the final coat of shellac has dried. Shellac comes in "white" and "orange." Both will deepen the color of a floor; the latter, which is an amber color, far more than the former. Shellac is put on with a brush.

■ Varnish: This also deepens the floor color. While much more durable than shellac, varnish is more difficult to use because it takes so long to dry. You must allow at least 24 hours' drying time between coats.

Varnish is impervious to alcohol but it scratches white and touch-ups cannot be made without their showing. Shellac, on the other hand, can be touched up by dissolving with alcohol and rebrushing.

■ Stain: This type of finish has come on strongly in the past few years. It works just like a stain for furniture. You wipe a liberal amount of it on the floor, let it dry a specified time (30 minutes, customarily), then wipe off most of it. A big advantage of stains is the impressive color change you can effect in a floor; stains are available in many wood tones and also in nonwood hues. Since stains are basically only colorings, however, they need protection. A coat of shellac, followed by waxing, provides this.

■ Penetrating wood finishes: These have always been among the best-wearing finishes, yet have had to contend with the public's partiality to

When one speaks of shellac, one speaks in terms of "pound cuts." This refers to the number of pounds of dry shellac dissolved in a single gallon of alcohol. For example, "4-pound cut shellac" is made by dissolving 4 pounds of shellac in a gallon of alcohol. Different jobs require different cuts. For most uses, however, a 3-pound cut will work best—floors are finished with this cut. Various shellac cuts can be bought ready-mixed at paint stores, or you can mix your own. Dealers have tables showing how, with correct proportions for specific uses.

Shellac can be useful in repairing cuts, nicks, and holes in wood. Other uses are priming nailheads and sealing knots (shown here) before applying a final coat of enamel or similar finish. For small jobs, a camel's-hair brush is good. With it, you brush on shellac smoothly and without waste. Right after use, clean the brush in ammonia and warm water.

"French polishing" gives wood a rich finish. First, cover with thin coat of 4-pound cut shellac, using lintless cloth wrapped around cotton. Let dry; sand lightly. Repeat until sheen appears. Then apply teaspoonful of shellac with 2 or 3 drops of boiled linseed oil. Put on several coats. Always apply with circular motion.

To repair a hole in wood, first scrape loose material out of hole with knife tip. Partly fill hole with plastic wood (sold in several wood hues at hardware stores). Let harden, then finish filling hole. Brush shellac in hole, following grain of wood; let dry. Apply a coat of paste wax, buffing it gently.

Short-cut French polish: pour a little 4-pound cut shellac in one container, some turpentine in another. Moisten cloth pad in turpentine, then in shellac, and spread on evenly with circular motion. A pleasing gloss is built up with several coats. Add a few drops of boiled linseed oil for final one.

Any kind of mark on a wall, or a knot in wood paneling, can be effectively sealed with shellac and thus be kept from bleeding through finish paint. Three-pound cut works best. Simply brush it on, making sure you cover marks entirely. If they are very wide, use a bigger brush or a rag. Work quickly. Shellac dries very fast—in about 10 minutes. Before you know it, it will be tacky.

a glossy finish before becoming popular. Today they are doing that.

Though tough, penetrating wood finishes are easy to apply. You swab, brush, or roll them on, let seep into the floor (the resins fill air spaces in the wood), then wipe off excess after half an hour or so. Two coats are usually enough. This type of finish comes in clear form and in colors.

In all cases—that is, no matter which floor finish you choose—follow the manufacturer's instructions on the can label. Makers' directions for applying their products may vary, even though the products fall into the general categories of shellac, varnish, and so on.

PANELING

Wood Panels Bring Richness And Excitement to Tired Rooms

Natural wood and hardboard paneling have become increasingly popular as home decorating materials—and they well deserve this popularity. Available in a wide range of rich wood colors and delicate color tones with molding and trim to match, the panels are easily installed by any home handyman with basic do-it-yourself skills. Factory-applied finishes generally make paneling a tough, durable, easy-to-clean, and long-lasting surface, and ensure that time, cleaning, and everyday living will not mar the natural beauty and warmth of the wood grains.

The colors, tones, grains, and finishes of plywood and hardboard paneling allow the decorator to achieve exactly the desired effect to suit a particular room or furniture style. And in addition to making the walls themselves an integral part of the room's decorating theme, these very tough materials frequently withstand a lot of abuse that would damage lesser walls—such as banging by door handles or furniture and roughhousing of the children.

The large panels go up fast, either by nailing or adhesive application. The prefinished surface is mostly resistant to scratching, abrasion, and staining. Maintenance is simple—just wipe the walls clean with a damp rag.

Solve decorating problems with paneling

Wall treatment can pose a real challenge for the decorator. Should the walls be plain or fancy, subtle or striking? Should they remain

At left, painted panels intermingled with the prefinished panels demonstrate how well painted and wood-grained surfaces blend. Background paneling is "Sturbridge" by *Armstrong.* The "Weathered timber" ceiling beams are actually of featherweight polyurethane by *Paeco-wood.* The panel at top left is "Royal Cherry" by *Evans;* the large panel in top grouping is "Brazilian Rosewood," a Royalcote product of *Masonite;* to the right are "Hickory" by *Georgia-Pacific* and, below it, "Barnside" by *U.S. Plywood.* Middle group includes "Ranchero" by *U.S. Plywood* and "Ceylon Teak" by *Masonite.* Large hardboard panel in the bottom grouping is *Abitibi's* "Avocado Pecan." At right is deep-toned "Walnut" paneling by *Georgia-Pacific.*

Straightforward charm is a tangible decorating element▶ in the living room at the right. Textural interest is provided by the rough stone fireplace and the soft homespun rug, and is highlighted by the roughhewn paneled wall of pecky cypress. All contrast with the polished glow of the furniture while a traditional documentary print is balanced by a coordinating plaid.

The rich wood tones, soft sheen, and rippling grain of prefinished Gothic oak paneling give this room elegance and dignity. Against this background, the unusual floor treatment, moorish arches, brass-and-ebony framed Japanese print, and brightly colored furniture present a startling contrast, creating an air of exotic luxury.

in the background, simply providing a setting? Should one of them be accented? Should they all stand out boldly as major elements in the room plan? Paneling can be the key to achieving whatever effect is desired.

The warm, rich beauty of wood-grain paneling gives any room in the home a feeling of luxury. Most frequently used in dens and family rooms, it is finding its way into living rooms, dining rooms, bedrooms, kitchens—even bathrooms. Its inherent adaptability can benefit just about any decorating scheme.

In addition to utilizing its elegant beauty and practicality as a wall-covering material, there are many unique effects that can be created through the use of paneling. Installing it on the ceiling—especially on a sloping, cathedral-type ceiling—adds a touch of drama and grandeur to a room. Doors can be covered with paneling, either to blend into the surrounding walls or to stand out as decorative elements themselves. Built-in drawers and cabinets faced with the same paneling as the walls can provide unobtrusive storage space for any room. Simple room dividers of paneling to match the walls can separate too-large rooms into distinct and intimate areas. Paneling an archway between two rooms draws interest to the opening. Or an accent wall can be covered with wood-grain paneling installed with the grooves running horizontally rather than vertically—an unusual, attention-getting treatment.

The diversity of paneling

The tremendous variety of paneling on the market makes it a great favorite with the astute decorator. Real wood paneling is available in very many of the 1100 or so woods native to this country as well as many of the exotics grown abroad, such as teak and Brazilian rosewood. While the intriguing and infinitely differing grain patterns of natural wood cannot truly be duplicated, hardboard manufacturers have devised technological processes that allow them to present a product that closely resembles the real thing. The imitation is in some ways superior, since it cannot splinter, split, or check and has sound-resistant qualities.

Not all wall paneling is of the wood-grain variety. Plastic-coated hardboard offers a full range of colors and a broad selection of patterns. Marble, tile, mosaic, or leather present endless possibilities to the home decorator.

Gold-shaded paneling in the room below provides a soft background and blends well with the gold tones of the floor covering and the chair fabric. The red of the sofa is continued in the russet-red trim molding, providing a perfect complement to the gold. Polished wood furniture adds to the warmth of the room.

Bleached wood paneling of the accent wall in the small living room below makes the area seem larger. It is well complemented by the storage-wall piece of antiqued pine, and provides a counterpoint to the room's bright colors and the plaid-covered sofa.

In the country room at the bottom, the random-plank paneling is whitewashed, as are ceiling beams and supporting posts, but the style comes through as bold and crisp because of the skillful blending of dashing red, white, and blue.

Prices of paneling

The price range of wall paneling is as wide as the choices available. To cover a 12-foot-long wall, you can spend more than $300—or under $15 (even less if you buy some types of unfinished paneling, but the cost, time, and mess involved in finishing it yourself generally makes this a poor choice). In terms of durability and easy maintenance, even the more expensive panelings must be rated among the best bargains.

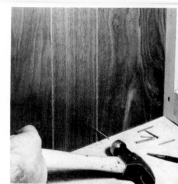

Do-it-yourself installation

Installation of wall paneling is relatively quick and easy, well within the capabilities of most do-it-yourself decorators. If the subsurface (a plaster- or gypsum-board wall, for example) is in good shape, panels can simply be glued to this with contact cement or special adhesive. But if the old wall is not plumb, or if there is loose and crumbling plaster or any other irregularity, furring strips should be applied to form a base for the paneling.

Horizontal furring strips should be placed at the top and bottom of the wall and at 16-inch intervals between; vertical strips are placed at corners and where panel joints occur. Fasten the 1x2 or 1x3 strips with 8d nails driven into wall studs and plates.

When a masonry wall is to be paneled, perforated anchor nails are applied with adhesive (1), then furring strips are driven onto the nails, which are clinched over. Paneling is then applied in the usual way. Nail through panels into furring (2); where nails are not covered by molding, they are countersunk and hidden by filler. Paneling may be applied directly to a sound wall surface. First, coat back of panel and bare wall with contact cement (3); let cement become tacky, then fit the panel carefully into place (4) and press it firmly. Reinforce the bond by nailing with small finishing nails along the top and bottom plates, and occasionally along the studs; measure to find stud centers (5). Some paneling materials are in plank form, with grooved and lipped edges into which metal clips fit to hold planks to furring and make a tight joint. Special grooved furring strips are nailed to the wall (6). The clips are inserted into the grooves with their flanges fitted over the lip of the plank (7). Clips are then nailed to the furring strips. The next plank is then slipped into place (8), fitting into the clips. The plank's top lip conceals the clips, and forms a neat V-joint with the neighboring plank.

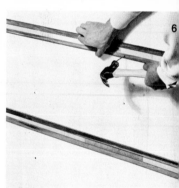

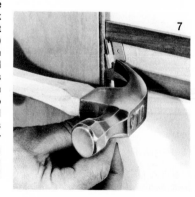

How To Join Corners

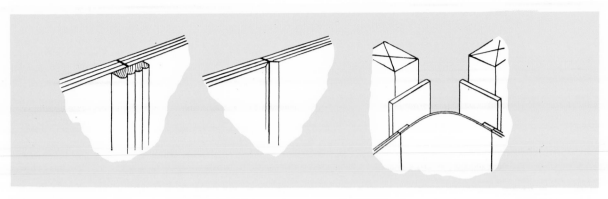

Joints and corners of plywood paneling can be handled in a number of different ways. The batten joint, left, is a butted joint covered with a molding strip to conceal any gaps. The V-joint, middle, has a bevel at the edge of each panel; this should not be cut deeper than the face veneer. At right is a veneer corner strip, a smooth, curved inside corner formed by a thin strip of matching veneer fastened to thin furring strips.

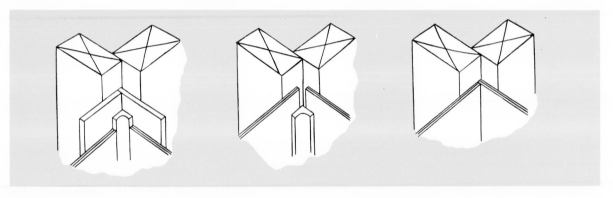

Inset cove molding, left, forms a rounded corner more easily and at less expense than a veneer strip. The molding is set in place first, then panels are butted against it. An even simpler way of finishing inside corners is to apply cove molding over the joint after the panels are in place, middle. Butt joint, right, is simplest of all—if the walls and the paneling are perfectly square. If, however, a gap shows, cove molding should be applied instead.

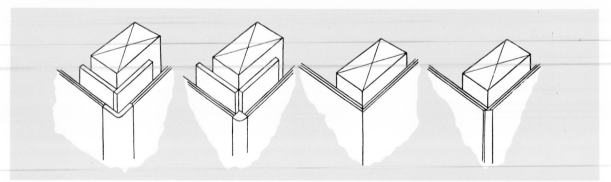

For outside corners, special veneer corner strips, left, may be purchased. These are attached first, then the panels are butted against them. Quarter-round molding, second from left, may also be used in the same manner; it should be set into the furring strips so that it does not project beyond the face of the paneling. Edges may also be mitered, second from right. Or edges may be butted and the sharp corner sanded down, right.

The paneling is then applied to the furring strips with adhesive or by nailing. If adhesive is used, it is advisable to drive nails along the top and bottom of each panel as insurance.

Hints on installation

Many wall paneling systems make allowances for joints between panels (tongue-and-groove, overlap, butted V-joint, clips) and at corners. But with some types of paneling, it is up to the designer to decide what sort of effect is desired.

Several possibilities are shown on the facing page. Simplest of all is to cover the joint or corner with a piece of molding to conceal any gaps or irregularities. Several types of moldings are available for this purpose.

Pine-paneled walls form the setting for the graceful, understated charm of this old New England bedroom design. A 36-inch-high wainscot is formed by installing the paneling with grooves running horizontally. Above that, grooves run vertically up to a molding at the ceiling line. The lightness of scale and proportion of the bed and chests is achieved by skillful and sensitive employment of turnings and spindles, batwing hardware, and H-L hinges. Chests rest on ogee feet; arched doors give a delightful rustic look. The furniture offers the charm of eighteenth-century detail and craftsmanship, but it is the wall paneling that truly sets the theme for this bedroom. Modern, prefinished paneling is a good choice for children's rooms, too. It is often tough enough to withstand the exuberance of youngsters at play; such things as crayon marks or jelly stains can usually be wiped off with a damp cloth.

Other methods of joining panels may require a bit more skill, and some presuppose that the subsurface to which the paneling is being applied is perfectly plumb and square. If this is not so, the joint will be imperfect.

Molding trim

A wide variety of wood moldings is available to trim both wood and hardboard wall paneling. Some of these are prefinished to match a specific paneling, eliminating on-the-job finishing. Others must be stained to the color of the paneling on the walls.

In addition to inside and outside corner moldings, there are baseboard and shoe moldings for use at the floor-wall joint; crown cove for use at the ceiling line; chair rail, installed horizontally at the top of wainscoting; and casing, trim, and stop moldings for use around door and window openings. All these moldings are nailed in place

The wall treatment on the facing page features portable hardboard units. These could be expanded to an entire wall simply by adding on in either direction. Construction details are shown below. The 2x6 uprights are slotted to receive alternating 16-inch wormy-chestnut panels and 6-inch walnut panels. The narrow vertical insets at the rear have fascia boards to hide small spotlight fixtures; adjustable glass shelves are also provided. The wider units are held together by strips at the back.

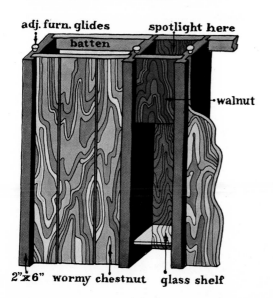

adj. furn. glides   spotlight here
batten
walnut
2"x6" wormy chestnut   glass shelf

Prefinished hardboard paneling is an excellent wall-covering material. It comes in just about any wood-grain pattern available, as well as a number of other colorful patterns. Installation is generally similar to that of wood paneling. The hardboard may be applied over a solid subsurface with adhesive. Because there is a certain amount of give to the panels, they can even be glued to slightly uneven walls; brace the panel by extending boards across to the opposite wall during the drying period. Horizontal boards protect the prefinished surface.

Over walls that are in poor condition or out of plumb, and over masonry walls, furring strips must be used as a base for the hardboard. These may be applied horizontally or vertically on 16-inch centers, as at right. The hardboard is then nailed to the furring strips or fastened with adhesive. Provide backing for the panels at all edges, and always nail perpendicular to the panel surface, starting at the center and working outward. Over furring strips or on open framing, hardboard must be at least 3/16-inch thick; thinner panels require solid backing.

Stock wood moldings can be used with hardboard paneling. Most panel manufacturers offer wood molding prefinished (and in some cases vinyl-coated) to match the paneling. PVC plastic moldings are also available to match many types of paneling, and a wide range of metal moldings can also be used. In addition to the outside corner molding shown at right, there are inside corners, dividers, edging, end caps, coves—a type for every need. Interesting design effects can be achieved by using contrasting moldings to provide accent lines on a wall.

Corner and joint treatment can be an important part of the overall wall decor —rather than trying to hide these areas, they can be pointed up as decorative assets. For example, at right, upholsterer's gimp of harmonizing color makes an attractive joint treatment for hardboard panels with a prefinished, textured, leatherlike surface. The gimp can be of leather or artificial leather, and the effect could be varied by using material of a different shade than the paneling. Hardboard panels of this type may be effectively used either on full walls or as wainscoting.

with 4d finishing nails; the nails are counter-sunk, and the holes filled with color-matched wood putty.

Choosing a suitable molding

Where should you use wall paneling? Any places in your home where it fits into your decorating scheme—and these will be many because of the inherent versatility and immense variety of types and patterns available.

Start with the family room, where the popularity explosion of paneling materials got its start. This most-lived-in room in the home demands a setting in keeping with its recreational-social activities. The walls should be vibrant in appearance, yet be able to withstand abuse from tiny-tot activity, toy impact, finger-marking, and the energy of teen-age swingers. It is also important that they should be easy to clean.

The family room is also a good place to install paneling that actually goes to work for you. Unfinished (then painted) pegboard panels can be fitted with a variety of shelf supports, hooks, and other hardware that allows you to display books, knickknacks, and family treasures—and store toys right on the walls. Some panels have holes from floor to ceiling; others have holes from ceiling down to wainscot, with random grooves from there to the floor; still others have slots to receive shelf brackets concealed in the random-width V-grooves. Shelves placed on these brackets support an amazingly heavy load.

Move into the living room—the showcase of your home's styling and its decorative focal point. Paneling's unparalleled diversity of colors, grains, and textures enables you to achieve a look of luxury and glamor. Choose among smooth-surfaced panels or those with rough-

Warm tones are important in your color planning. The family room at the left gains a pleasing unity from the beauty of the wood paneling, floors, and furniture. The walnut paneling provides a restrained background for sparkling colors in the furnishings. Plenty of shelf space and cabinet storage is a bonus.

The wood-paneled wall with traditional molding trim forms a rich setting for the classic furniture styles in the living room below. The color scheme is basically simple. An off-white Empire sofa blends with rug and drapery; wing chair repeats color of end wall.

A successful blending of a diversity of decorating elements is seen in the small corridor-plan kitchen and dinette area at the left. The wall paneling is pickled cypress, a light textured wood complementing the soft warm tones of the maple cabinets, which are matched by the refrigerator at the right. The countertop is white plastic laminate. The slate floor and the ceiling of patterned wallpaper (carried down onto the soffit) tie the two areas together. The cozy dining grouping includes an old Spanish church pew, modern bucket chairs, a slate-topped table, and an antique Tiffany-glass shade on the hanging fixture.

The bathroom has become the jewel of the home and is an important element in the overall decorating scheme. Paneling is an ideal material for use in this room. Bold exotic wood grains, rich marble reproductions, fleeces, tapestries, and many other unusual designs allow you to create the effect you desire. In the bathroom below, impressionistic wallpaper is augmented by rich green paint on rough "barn-siding" panels. Furniture-styled accessories specially designed for the bathroom have an antique gold finish. Open storage shelves add bright colors.

sawn, distressed, or fissured surfaces; wood grains of bold figuration or subtle tones; colors that blend with any decor. There are also exotic finishes in marble effects; embossed patterns: diamond, louvered, wicker, burlap, flocked, striated; lacy prints; tapesty; and solid decorator colors.

You may not wish to panel the entire living room, but consider doing an accent wall or walls. You might do one wall in a mix-match— a marbleized or solid-color prefinished hardboard paneling along with a wood grain. Or one wall could be faced with a tapestry panel and the adjoining wall in wood grain. Combinations are many, but select wisely.

Similar combinations or accenting can be employed in the dining room to give it an air of formal elegance. In a home with a living-dining area, different types of wall paneling can give a sense of separation to the two areas without closing them off from one another.

The modern kitchen should be cheerful and serviceable, with a minimum of maintenance required. Today's appliances, cabinets, and other kitchen furnishings are styled to make this another impressive room. As a backdrop for this equipment and a decorating element in itself, paneling is in perfect taste.

You can choose a wood grain to blend with the cabinets, or a solid-color hardboard to complement the appliances, or one of the many other patterned panels that fit any architectural styling. Here again, perforated panels may be used for the display and storage of utensils.

In the bathroom, the clinical look has been supplanted by colors and patterns reflecting a more sophisticated atmosphere. Plastic-coated hardboard panels are a practical way to indulge in a flair for the unusual in bathroom decor.

Paneling played an important role in the fireplace-updating project below. First, the entire fireplace—bricks, mantel, and all—was painted flat black. The wall above was then furred out and rosewood paneling was glued in place. The furring strips that showed at the edges of the paneling were painted black. At the top of the paneling, a light box was framed and covered with the same paneling. A fluorescent light with diffuser panels highlights the grain.

The use of paneling is not limited to any specific areas. While the walls of rooms are the most logical for such treatment, even hallways and stair-sides are eligible, as shown here. This wooden stairway is beautifully set off by its background of odd-board paneling, properly "distressed" to indicate age and weathering, and by the shaggy stair carpet that matches other accessories.

This simply furnished family room is a natural for relaxed, casual entertaining. The walls are paneled with wide lengths of elm, with lovely wavy grain and honey-gold tones that add texture and lightness to the room. The wood walls, weather-bleached antique beams, and dark floors all contribute to the room's rustic atmosphere.

Designing and Equipping This Major Storage Area

If the word "pantry" conjures up in your mind a musty, cavernous array of cupboards in which your grandmother stored her watermelon pickle and crocks of ginger cookies, you are emotionally ready to sing the virtues of pantries. The symphony of smells: pungent, mysterious spices; the fragrance of home-baked bread and cookies; the tantalizing aroma of coffee—all of these made the pantry in former days a treasure trove of delights. The pantry was the cook's security blanket: from it came the extra jars of spiced peaches and green beans needed to fill out the menu when an unexpected guest came to call.

Tall, skinny pantry units take up little space in a kitchen, yet hold an amazing number of staples. Four units, or drawers, are shown to the left. Each glides in and out to reveal a variety of cans and boxes, stored one deep. Every item is clearly visible and easily accessible. Each unit is 12 inches wide, and each has a perforated hardboard divider on either side of which are mounted adjustable shelves. The stack of four units is positioned here to act as a room divider. For added utility, their sides could be hung with pegboard panels or with a bulletin board or a blackboard. Adhesive labels on the outside of the units, describing the contents of the shelves, would be useful in homes where several people use the pantry.

Modern pantries

Times are different now. The modern housewife has a freezer and not many canned fruits and vegetables. Her shopping habits are different, too. However, many houses still have actual pantries, and the best of them are just as exciting and filled with resources for the creative cook as in former days.

Recently, newer houses have been built without the separate room or closet that can be strictly termed a pantry. In many cases, however, the newer homes provide "in-kitchen" areas that can be loosely considered as pantries, or they have space that may be converted to such use. It is the proper functional use of that space which transmutes a storage area into a pantry.

Putting together a pantry

Like kitchens, pantries must be carefully planned and executed in order to save time, motion, and energy. They are workrooms as well as storage rooms. Whatever a pantry's size, it will benefit from an analysis of its function as it affects its users.

If the storage room for food is extremely limited in your kitchen, and if it does not seem possible to build additional shelves or cupboards, you might consider an "auxiliary pantry" in your basement. Inexpensive, easy-to-assemble steel shelves will hold cases of canned goods and paper supplies. If they are combined with an auxiliary freezer, you will be ready for whatever emergency arises.

Pantry supplies include items as varied in size as tiny jars of spices and gallon jugs of cooking oil. If you try to store everything on standard shelves, you will waste space. Investi-

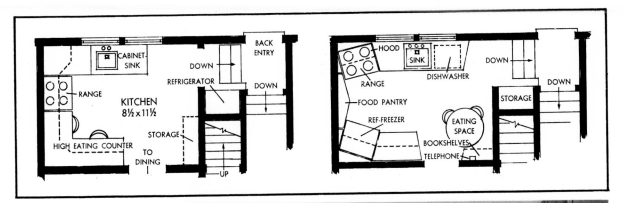

Above: before remodeling, kitchen lacked storage space; refrigerator was placed far from actual work area; eating counter had to double as an area for food preparation. Result was a cramped, inefficient room. After remodeling, appliances were angled to permit space for a tiny, triangular pantry; cabinets were built above the appliances and at an angle to the wall. Economizing on space even left room for a small eating area and a new dishwasher.

Tiny but efficient pantry is located at the blind end of a narrow kitchen. Angling appliances away from the wall created more working space near the pantry. Storage space was gained because pantry is triangular, extending into the room. Adjustable shelves are 11 inches at their widest, tapering to a width of 4 inches at each end—wide enough to hold everything from cereal boxes to slim bottles of spice. Everything in pantry is stored one deep, so all items are in full view.

gate racks and expanding stair-type shelves that
fit on regular shelves and double or triple your
storage area. They also allow you to stack cans
so labels can be read. Adjustable shelves are
helpful in providing space for tall items like
cereal boxes, and smaller openings for flat boxes
of spaghetti or cookies.

Organizing your pantry

Plan your pantry area to fit the person who uses
it most; do not store everyday items on high
shelves if the cook is short. Some homemakers
prefer everything out in the open and visible;
others like things tucked away out of sight for
an uncluttered look.

No matter what your storage method, try
to have a "filing system" so you can find items
by type—all spices in one area, soup cans on
one turntable, and all snack foods together.

Keep one area for "guests"—a shelf that includes easy-to-fix dips and nibble foods, drink
mixes, pâté, fancy cookies, and other between-
meal snacks. Add tins of ready-to-heat foods
such as chicken, chili, stews, hearty soups,
canned bacon, and other foods that will make it
easy to prepare a simple supper unexpectedly.

Have a pad and pencil or blackboard near
your pantry area so that, as you start using the
last of any item, you can jot down on a shopping
list a reminder to repurchase.

Storage in this walk-in pantry reaches to the ceiling, and
although the shelves are not wide enough to store items
two-deep, there is still ample space for dry staples, canned
foods, vegetables, cooking utensils, and electric appliances. Folding doors conceal the pantry, which has its
own lighting—a globe overhead and a fluorescent installation over the Plastic-covered work space. Two helpful
additions here would be a step ladder, and a shelf for
cookbooks. For safety's sake, in a pantry like this, heavy
items should be stored below head level.

Another walk-in pantry triples its storage space by using
swinging doors equipped with deep storage shelves.
Shelves in the main area are adjustable, on tracks, and
wide enough for items to be stored four deep. Overhead
lighting makes everything clearly visible. Large pantries
like this one cut down on trips to the market.

Check your pantry regularly to reevaluate its utility. You will save money by eliminating items that just "sit there"; others, you will discover, are used often enough to justify the purchase of jumbo economy sizes.

You can provide more space for food and food-preparation items if you relegate cleaning supplies to your cleaning closet, and if bathroom supplies are stored in the bathroom, and laundry supplies next to your washer and dryer.

Keeping the pantry up-to-date

Analyze your food purchases and you will readily see that food storage space must be cap-

The ingeniously designed pantry above, with slide-out shelves and drawers, is easy to make. Basically a big box, it can be built of birch or other hardwood plywood, or of inexpensive fir. A door closes over the front of the unit.

A built-in pantry closet, part of a series of similar built-ins, takes full advantage of the maximum possible storage area, and provides for the greatest accessibility. The outward-swinging door has its own shelves, the contents protected by edges from falling off. Note how the two sets of shelves mesh when the pantry is closed.

The pantry below is part of the decorating scheme of a bright modern house. Open shelves hold packages that seem to match the vivid abstract painting hung above the pots-and-pans board. Keeping utensils and supplies in sight is timesaving, but spend some of that time to restore order frequently. Neatness makes a big difference.

Concealed behind double folding doors, this center, right, was built near the family dining room, making it possible to serve complete meals there with maximum convenience. Cupboards hold supplies and serving accessories. Counter includes sink, icemaker, and backsplash, and enough electrical outlets to handle small appliances for counter-cooking. Two ceiling spotlights illuminate the area.

This mini-pantry features space-saving 5-inch-deep shelves, just wide enough for cans and bottles. When planning your pantry, remember that space can be saved by making depth of shelves to fit standard sizes of boxes, bottles, and cans. Organization of shelves should be determined by frequency of use, and heavy articles should never be placed precariously. Every pantry should include a child-proof latch.

This refreshment pantry, below, was once a cleaning closet. Situated next to living-dining area, it was converted to a pantry to take advantage of its convenient location. The closet door was replaced with folding louvered doors, making total cabinet space accessible. When planning or remodeling pantries, be sure your lighting level is adequate for reading labels, mixing, serving, locating anything.

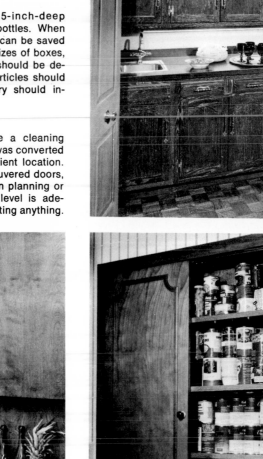

This compact, carefully organized kitchen almost eliminates the need for a pantry. Often-used cooking ingredients are decoratively stored within easy reach of cook. Pans and utensils are also conveniently located, in drawers beneath countertop.

When the doors of the 5x7-foot pantry, left, are opened, an automatic light reveals many storage shelves. Racks to hold small items line the backs of the doors. The doors are stock items at any lumberyard; they measure 2'6"x6'8"

able of handling a variety of shapes and sizes. Every family, however, tends to follow a pattern of proportion in its buying habits—so many cans, so many tall boxes, so many jars, and so forth.

Tailor your storage space to suit your own family's needs. There are many items on the market that can aid you in organizing the storage areas of your pantry: plastic dishpans, adjustable racks, shelves, straw baskets, pegboards, metal dividers, and pullout drawers.

PAPER PROJECTS

Use Paper to Decorate
Useful Articles for Home and Gifts

Paper craft is not new. It has been popular in the Orient for centuries, and during the seventeenth century in Europe and the nineteenth century in America, elegant papier-mâché tables, chairs, trays, and boxes were much in vogue. These articles, of macerated paper molded and glued into shape, were usually finished with black lacquer and sometimes inlaid with mother-of-pearl. Collectors search for them now, and examples can be seen in museums here and abroad. Our modern paper articles, ranging from furniture to clothing, may be bought in specialty shops, or the amateur can learn to make them himself. He has the ad-

vantage of today's abundant packaging and new, strong adhesives to simplify his work. Even children can make the easier things and are often very good at the craft, since most of them are taught to work with paper in their early school years. Several projects are shown and described on this and the following pages. Because of the recent emphasis on recycling paper, paper crafts are enjoying a resurgence of popularity in America. Papier-mâché, a craft material that has been almost universally used for twenty centuries, is an especially rewarding way for the homemaker to recycle the paper and cardboard that accumulate in her home. Papier-

The cube tables in this cheerful setting can be constructed quite easily from strong cardboard boxes such as those in which canned and bottled goods are shipped. Your neighborhood dealers will be glad to give them to you. If necessary, you can strengthen the tables by gluing the joints. Then paint or lacquer them to suit your color scheme. Decorate with decalcomanias, your own artwork, or pictures clipped from magazines. Any appliquéd decoration will be more secure if it is coated with colorless lacquer.

Children's cardboard chairs, similar to those shown here, ▶ can be purchased in stores that specialize in paper products. But if you can find some large, sturdy cartons, you can make them. Leftover wallpaper or vinyl wall covering makes an excellent outer finish. The chairs need not match, so you can use odds and ends. They are so lightweight that even children can move and handle them easily, and they are just the thing for a room like this, which is planned for use by all members of the family. Cardboard chairs would also be excellent for a weekend house, especially a rented one that perhaps is not too well equipped. The other furnishings of the rooms are equally flexible. The lounge pads could double for sleeping an overnight guest or two—fun for youngsters. The boxes on the wall, for books, toys, and other not-too-heavy things, could be cardboard cartons or boxes or wooden crates nailed to the wall.

mâché consists of a mash made from wheat paste and/or white glue and strips of paper. The mash can be layered over a light form (styrofoam is particularly good for this), molded, or shaped to create anything from puppets and puppet theatres, candlesticks, masks, mobiles, center-pieces, mirror frames, lamp bases, and jewelry to banks, bowls, artificial fruit, trays, sculpture, and Christmas tree decorations.

When one thinks of paper craft, two countries immediately come to mind: Japan and Mexico. Japan is the origin of a number of exciting paper

For this Mexican setting, your tablecloth can be runners of crepe paper in any mixture of bright colors, as pictured here, or your white cloth with a crepe-paper runner down the center. The candleholders are inexpensive little funnels set into cardboard tubes (the kind inside a roll of paper towels would be fine). Then spray with silver paint to resemble Mexican tin. Or, if you have some plain candleholders, they can be wrapped in silver foil to give them the tin look. Even small tin cans would do. Their decorations can be pocket mirrors framed in fringed foil or in colored crepe paper cut for a fringed look. Paper flowers in a multitude of colors can be made in several sizes, some to stand in a low vase, others to be arranged around its base. You can also intersperse the flowers with real leaves; most appropriate are those that dry well, such as magnolia, eucalyptus, and evergreens.

creations: paper-covered, lacquered umbrellas; paper-covered screens; paper lanterns; papier-mâché wallets and boxes; kites; masks; huge folding paper decorations; even paper dragons. All are decorated in the inimitable Japanese fashion; all are splendid additions to nearly any room. Also from Japan comes the wonderful art of origami—intricately folded paper objects that include folding flowers and birds with movable wings. Origami papers and instructions can be purchased at art stores and Oriental shops. Because of their bright colors, origami papers are excellent materials for other craft projects, such as collages.

Mexico, of course, produces those enormous, vividly colored paper flowers. In addition to flowers, Mexican papier-mâché objects are especially delightful. Each year hundreds of Mexican papier-mâché creations—trees of life, votive items, candlesticks, toys, and masks—are imported to the United States. Perhaps the most popular paper product of Mexico is the *pinata,* a traditional Christmas treat. Made from papier-mâché and brightly colored tissue paper covering a thin ceramic base, pinatas are filled with candy and presents, and are made in fascinating shapes: fierce bulls, elegant ladies, clowns, and flowers. In addition to being the star attraction at parties (blindfolded guests hit at them until they are broken and release their hidden treats), pinatas are wonderful decorative items and, like Japanese kites, are very impressive when hung from the ceiling.

Mexico and Japan do not have a monopoly on paper crafts, however: Polish cut-paper ornaments are famous throughout Europe; Russian papier-mâché products are popular U.S. imports; and miniature papier-mâché boxes, beautifully painted and brightly colored, are imported by the thousands to the U.S. from the Near East and India.

Now that artificial flowers have come into their own and can be fashioned of many different papers, from crepe or tissue to newspapers or grocery bags, there is a whole new scope for

The first step in making quite large paper flowers like these is cutting a package of crepe paper in half horizontally, or across the grain. For smaller flowers, cut it in thirds or quarters. Then shape the petals as shown, rounding or pointing one side or snipping at about ⅛-inch intervals for daisy-like petals. A straightened-out wire coat hanger, or any wire about that thick, will do for the stems. You can make the flowers with or without centers and can vary stem length.

The petals can now be molded by gently stretching the center of each, and the ends can be slightly curled. Gather the petals around the stem in a circular fashion, as a flower is formed; or gather them in your hand as you build up the flower. Then fasten the part to be attached to the stem with a single strand of picture wire or any very fine wire. For your first try at paper flowers, study real and artificial flowers and do a little experimenting.

Attach the flower to coat hanger or wire, as shown. The calyx of green leaves is optional, but can be cut from crepe paper. Now wrap the flower to the stem with green masking or florist's tape. The stem can be covered with masking tape or strips of green crepe paper. For this process, hold the stem in your left hand, the covering in your right; then turn the stem with your left hand, as shown, until it is thoroughly wrapped. Fasten with a bit of masking tape.

As with any craft, one learns as one works; eventually it is possible to produce a great assortment of flowers like those in this group. Materials for making them are available in shops that sell crepe and tissue paper. Some shops also sell kits containing all the requirements of paper, wire, tape, and glue. Methods for producing the flowers and arrangements vary. In some cases, each petal (notably those that are rather flat) is glued to the stem, and the flower is constructed that way. Tissue paper, which comes in a marvelous spectrum of colors, may be used instead of crepe paper, although it is more delicate and therefore more difficult to handle. Flower centers can be little clusters of paper, tiny dried flowers, or dried seed pods, in a darker shade than the petals.

them not only in the dining room but throughout the house. To make paper flowers, follow the directions on the preceding page. Once you have mastered these basic instructions, you will soon develop paper objects of your own, pretty enough for displaying in your home and for giving to your friends.

Easy frames for mirrors

The materials required for framing these or other mirrors are gift wrap or wallpaper, cardboard, strong plastic tape, clear spray lacquer, and single-edged razor blades. The sketches below illustrate the process. A, B, C are the three pieces of cardboard to be cut into the shape you wish—one for the frame, one to hold the mirror, and the third as backing. In cutting the paper for the frame, allow 1 inch all around to turn

A collection of mirrors can be framed in gift wrap or wallpaper, scraps of which you may have on hand—each mirror requires only a small amount. You may even have an extra mirror or two around. The final shape depends on how you cut and form the frame. These make excellent gifts and are popular with the younger set. There is no limit to the ways you can frame and trim even large mirrors.

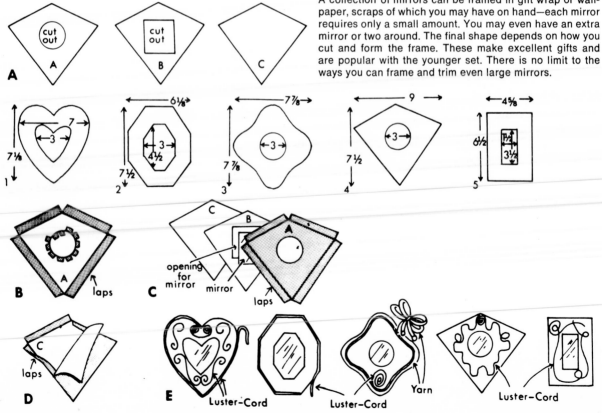

Three useful accessories for your home or for a friend: a ladybug bulletin board, a portfolio for writing materials, and a wastebasket. All are covered with self-adhesive paper. Children usually enjoy working on projects such as these, and can do most of the ones shown here (as well as mirror frames) with only a little assistance.

back; secure with glue as in figure B. Measurements given here can be adjusted to a mirror of any size. Figure D shows how to join the parts and how to trim with yarn or ribbon.

For the bulletin board, portfolio, and wastebasket at left, you will need one sheet of giftwrap paper or an equivalent amount of wallpaper for each; a piece of 1/4-inch cork or heavy canvas; corrugated board or heavy cardboard; colorless glue; spray paint; some fine wire on which to wrap the wool-yarn trimming; two adhesive eyelets; two small picture hooks; picture wire. Follow steps A, B, C, D for assembling.

For the wastebasket, you can use a metal or paper basket that needs refurbishing or a large tub like those sold in paint stores. If you wish, or if the basket is not in too good condition, spray the inside and rim with colorless lacquer, and make a cardboard sleeve, as in sketch G. H and I show how to apply paper cover and trim. The portfolio is merely white cardboard and decorative paper. First, cut a cardboard rec-

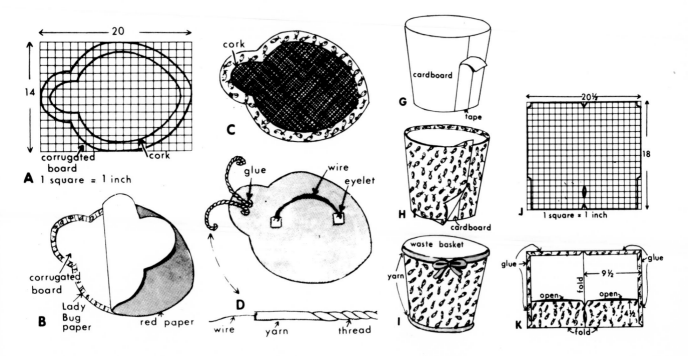

Pictured here, a cardboard collection for the skilled craftsman as well as for the novice who would like to become one. From left to right: the graceful pedestal, of corrugated board, is somewhat difficult to achieve. Its form combines complex curves and cunning folds as well as decorative inset lozenges of smooth brown paper. It is topped with brown paper flowers. Place mats, of plain and corrugated cardboard, also are finished with brown paper flowers. The corrugated-board candlesticks go well with the mats, and both table accessories are quite easily contrived. Above them is a frame for a mirror or picture, which can be made with all corrugated board or with corrugated and plain cardboard. So can the square wastebasket and the tall flower stand. The color of these boards is usually deep beige, and the neutral tone blends unobtrusively with all the other colors in a room. Because cardboard's main quality is texture, working with it is not complicated by color.

tangle (figure J, p. 2457). Then glue decorative paper to the cardboard and fold as in figure K. You can make the portfolio any size. The scale shown here is 1 square to the inch.

Artistic efforts

For anyone who has always longed to be a sculptor, the articles on these pages are a good introduction to modeling useful and decorative forms. All are made of cardboard, corrugated and plain, which constantly finds its way into your home or can be acquired without cost at your local stores. We suggest that you begin this paper craft with the simpler objects, such as the place mats and candleholders, since the principle for putting them together applies to even the more elaborate pieces. The latter are all built on an armature or base of plain cardboard held together with plastic tape. After that, the corrugated or plain facing is attached with a strong adhesive. You will need some sharp, single-edged razor blades to cut the board cleanly. The candleholders are shaped from four rectangular pieces for the base, four somewhat triangular pieces for the stems, and just a collar of corrugated board for the top. The mats are, obviously, rectangles of plain cardboard, trimmed with corrugated bands and flowers. You could round the corners for oval mats.

How to Lay Out and Improve Your Parking Space

When Mr. Homeowner goes to work in the morning, he probably goes by car. When his wife goes shopping, she very likely drives too. Perhaps their son has his own car, lovingly rebuilt from a near-wreck status. When visitors come, they usually arrive by car, and delivery-men and repairmen drive up in trucks. Every one of these people must have a place to park his vehicle, particularly if he lives in a community in which on-street parking is banned.

Not so long ago, a driveway meant a short private road between the garage and the street. Houses built 40 or more years ago usually have a garage in the back. New houses generally have driveways either in front of or to the side of the plot. A well-planned driveway includes, at the very least, an ample turnaround space and enough off-the-street parking to accommodate the needs of the householders.

These features require a good deal of space—typically a thousand square feet at a minimum. Since these areas must be flat, level, and un-obstructed, many of them end up looking dull and utilitarian. In order to be attractive, a drive-way/parking area must be integrated into the design of the house and grounds.

◄ A landscaped driveway in a minimum of space, left, manages to provide off-street parking space for three cars. The arrangement here is a little crowded—a car parked as shown blocks the turnaround. Also, when three cars are parked in front of this house, it would be difficult to enter the garage. However, when house and garage fill the width of the lot, as here, and are built close to the street, an arrangement of this general type is unavoidable.

When your plot provides sufficient space, a generous parking and turnaround area can do double duty as a paved deck for outdoor sports. At the same time, the carport—with the addition of comfortable outdoor furniture —can become a shaded luncheon patio. The arrangement above provides room for two cars under the carport, for the white car shown, and for a fourth one next to it, leaving plenty of turnaround room for all four vehicles.

In this unusual arrangement, two garages are set at the front of the property, the house's main entrance having been recessed between them. Each garage has a short apron, which provides parking space for one car: the aprons are connected to form a miniature square-U drive that also serves as a turnaround. The layout is simple, neat, and attractive; the centering of the planting in front has put an effective frame around the house's entry court. In some respects, however, it is a little too compact for maximum convenience: a car parked on either apron will block the entrance to one of the garages, and at the same time defeat the turnaround. Visitors—particularly delivery-men and maintenance men—tend to take advantage of off-street parking. This driveway plan means that one of the garages will often be blocked.

A functionally designed, small but uncrowded driveway and parking area is shown at left. There is adequate temporary parking for two cars parallel to the curb in front of the house. Although these cars would reduce the maneuvering space a little, the drive is fully the width of two cars at that point so there is room to drive past them. Even with two cars temporarily parked, there would be no difficulty in getting into the garage or using the turnaround. This drive has something of a slope, which poses several problems: first, it is necessary to establish a level area (or as nearly so as possible) for the parking of cars in order to minimize the strain on the brakes of the parked car, and the consequent possibility of a runaway. Second, the sloped surface imposes restrictions on the material used for the driveway. Only asphalt can be employed here.

Locations

Parking areas must be convenient for members of the family, guests, deliverymen, and repairmen. Parking areas should be large enough to accommodate several vehicles at once.

What is the best location for your parking area? The most logical area is the best. Driveway/parking areas can be situated either in front of the house, in back of the house, or on either side of it, depending upon the space available. If the driveway/parking area is to be located at the side of the house, an area at least 10 feet wide is necessary.

A modern driveway/parking area provides a paved surface that can support the weight of the cars that will be parked on it. It should be properly designed in relationship to the house and grounds so that the entire area is unified and attractive. The layout and placement of the driveway/parking area should also contribute .to the outdoor living arrangements.

If the door to your kitchen is at the back of your house and widely separated from your front door, your driveway should be so arranged as to offer easy access to both doors.

This parking area, upper left, is not paved, since the bare ground is capable of handling the relatively light traffic expected here. In the absence of a clearly defined paved surface, some other means must be used to distinguish the driveway area from the rest of the property. Here a combination of slat fencing and log bumpers has been employed. The logs, cut from the surrounding woods, and the cedar fence blend well with the natural sylvan setting. A paved area would look distractingly out of place on this property. To add a touch of color, fuchsias have been placed in cedar tubs at the end of the log barrier.

Unless a curb or bumper of some sort is placed between the paved parking area and the surrounding plantings, the plants run the risk of being crushed by the occasional careless driver. Bumpers can be attached to posts set in the paving material, as at left, or they can simply be thick planks (4 inches or more) bolted to the pavement. For temporary use—as at large parties, when more parking space than usual is needed—a large, heavy plank or squared-off log can be placed where needed. The front (or rear) of a parked automobile may extend 3 feet beyond the wheels, so give plants plenty of clearance.

The driveway area, left, is distinctly utilitarian—it has not been laid out to look like a play area—but its excellent design gives it the elegance of a piece of fine precision machinery. The parking and maneuvering areas, in brown-tinted concrete, are set off from the walkways, executed in a random mosaic of light-colored stones. The two textures and colors are a perfect complement to the color and design of the house. There is ample room for another car to park beside the one shown without blocking access to the carport at the right. Two cars can be parked in front of the house below without interfering with access to the garage or turnaround. The two lamps flanking the entrance are not only decorative—they shed light on the nearby portion of the driveway for the convenience of night visitors and members of the family returning home after dark.

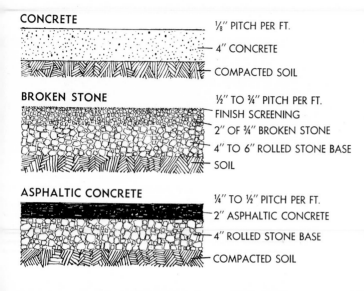

CONCRETE
- ⅛" PITCH PER FT.
- 4" CONCRETE
- COMPACTED SOIL

BROKEN STONE
- ½" TO ¾" PITCH PER FT.
- FINISH SCREENING
- 2" OF ¾" BROKEN STONE
- 4" TO 6" ROLLED STONE BASE
- SOIL

ASPHALTIC CONCRETE
- ¼" TO ½" PITCH PER FT.
- 2" ASPHALTIC CONCRETE
- 4" ROLLED STONE BASE
- COMPACTED SOIL

Choosing a location

There are several techniques for locating your driveway logically and for adapting one that is not located where you wish it was.

For example, if you do not want your driveway to run past your house, build the garage *next* to the house—and have it open in back as well as in front. If your driveway does pass your house, build a second-floor sun deck over that portion nearest your residence. Or you can make the driveway so attractive—by means of proper landscaping and an interesting surface material—that you will not want to hide it.

Having the driveway run around to the back of the house offers two practical advantages: access for deliveries, and more space for parking. Most deliveries can be better accommodated at the back door than at the front. The shorter the distance from car to kitchen, the less of a chore is bringing in the groceries. There may be plenty of space in front of your house for all necessary off-street parking. If there is not, or if the cars would be better out of sight behind the house, then a backyard parking area makes sense. Designed properly, it can double as a basketball court or party area.

On a very narrow lot, there may not be sufficient room to run the driveway past the house to the back. In that case, maneuvering and parking space must be provided in the front. If the house is set well back from the street, that will present no problem; but if not, it may be a real challenge to provide an adequate driveway area.

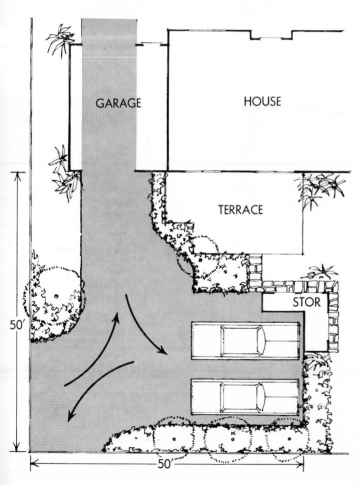

GARAGE   HOUSE

TERRACE

STOR

50'

50'

The drawing, above left, shows sectional views of three typical paving surfaces. Broken stone is the least expensive and the simplest. It presents only one problem for the home craftsman: rolling it heavily enough. If a lawn roller is the heaviest tool available, the material should be spread in several thin layers, each 2 inches or less. Each layer should be rolled six to eight times. Concrete can be laid by the home handyman if he has had experience using it. Asphalt requires special machinery that generally only a contractor has. On the lot diagrammed at left the parking and maneuvering area is in the rear. It is reached through a garage with a door at each end. If desired, a light roof can be built over the two-car parking area, converting it into a carport.

The wide, curving driveway, above, together with the elaborate pillared entrance, suggests the carriage drives of an earlier era. The resemblance is apt—those carriage drives existed partly because streets were not wide enough to park on in those days. The guests at a large dinner or ball had to park in the driveway. This drive provides parking space for four modern "carriages."

The unusual design, right, combines parking and play ▶ areas by stacking them on top of each other. This layout is particularly appropriate for a steeply sloping lot. The 20-feet-square carport accommodates two cars, and its location makes the back of it convenient to the kitchen. Guest cars, parked behind the family cars in the carport, are close to the front door.

Layout and dimensions

The particular layout chosen for a driveway and parking area should depend on the amount of space available and on the kind of facilities required. If the property offers enough room, the paved area should be interspersed with planted—or otherwise landscaped—areas. These add visual interest and serve to direct the flow of traffic in efficient patterns. Even if the available space leaves no room for plantings or other interruptions, the traffic patterns should be planned in advance so that the paved area can be shaped and trimmed to facilitate movement.

There are certain minimum dimensions for an area that is to be driven over. For a straight stretch wide enough for one car, where no backing up will be required, the absolute minimum is 8 feet. Nine feet is better, and 10 feet will be required for large cars. For a simple curve, the minimum radius is 18 feet inside, 29 feet outside. A turnaround Y should be at least 32 feet deep. Spaces for curbside parking should be 24

feet long and 8 feet wide; for head-in parking, they should be 20 feet long and 10 feet wide.

All of these dimensions are minimum ones. If the spaces are wider, they will be correspondingly easier to use. Although a homeowner has plenty of opportunity to learn the quirks of his driveway, no matter how cramped or difficult it is, impatient deliverymen in their large trucks and guests arriving after dark may damage their vehicles and your property.

Materials and construction

The first requirement of a driveway is that it be strong enough to take the steady traffic of the family car or cars and other vehicles, including an occasional heavy truck (such as an oil- or coal-delivery truck). Driveway strength depends not only on the construction of the paved area, but also on the nature of the ground underneath. If the soil is a soft clay or loam, and if good drainage is not provided, the paved surface will not be well supported when the ground is wet. Even a well-made concrete driveway, if it is heavily loaded under such conditions, will crack badly. A driveway made of aggregate material, such as crushed stone, will not crack. But it will develop ruts and potholes in wet weather, and these must later be filled in. Where a driveway is built over soft soil, adequate drainage is essential.

There are three basic types of material from which driveways can be made: crushed stone or similar loose material, blacktop (asphalt or asphaltic concrete), and solid concrete. Broken

The hedge and the grassy island, to the left, give this drive a figure-8 shape and provide plenty of room for maneuvering. At the same time, there is room for at least two cars to park in front of the house without affecting access to either the carport or the garage. Additional parking space is available, if needed.

The driveway shown in the plan above is pictured at right. The perspective is somewhat misleading: the driveway extends around behind the island, between it and the garage. A corner of the hedge appears in left foreground.

A strategically placed mound of soil, called a berm, is used, below, to add visual interest to an otherwise flat lot. It also conceals a large expanse of the carport's wall. In the front corner of a corner lot, the berm fills the center of a curving drive that gives access to both streets. The home's entrance is beneath the carport, which protects visitors from bad weather.

stone is the least expensive, and it is also the least solid. It has no structural strength of its own, simply transmitting the weight of the car to the ground beneath. It also requires the most maintenance, in the form of occasional leveling and the replacement of surface material. This material tends to be picked up when snow is shoveled off the driveway. It shows up in spring scattered on the grass along the edge.

Concrete, on the other hand, is completely rigid. It offers a great deal of structural strength, but it must be firmly and uniformly supported from underneath with foundation layers properly laid down. It can be tinted a variety of colors and is relatively simple to install, once the ground (if suitable at all) has been given the proper preparation.

Blacktop—asphalt or asphaltic concrete—represents a compromise in rigidity between the other two. Its flexibility makes it less prone to crack under excessive loads; if its underlying support weakens, it will bend instead of breaking.

Unlike concrete, asphalt can usually be repaired or restored if damaged. Some types of asphalt tend to soften and become sticky in hot weather—these should be avoided in home-driveway construction. Asphalt must be laid over a supporting layer of broken stone, heavily rolled. Its installation is a two-step operation, somewhat more complicated than concrete.

Driveways may also be constructed of other materials, such as pebble-textured aggregate concrete or bricks. These offer about the same structural advantages as ordinary concrete, but they are more interesting to look at—and, of course, more expensive.

Plantings and lights

Bushes planted along the sides of a driveway must be placed far enough back not to encroach

The attractive and practical driveway shown here provides all the basic necessities: off-street parking for two cars, plenty of turnaround space, and a stopping place at the entry. Artful landscaping has integrated these facilities into an aesthetically functional entry plaza. The sketch below shows the driveway paved with blacktop, but you could also use tinted concrete or aggregate concrete.

on driveway space. Pruning is not a satisfactory alternative; it produces sharp twigs capable of damaging a car's finish. Set strips of garden back far enough to avoid having drivers inadvertently back over them.

Driveway night-lighting is for safety; there must be enough of it and it must be in the right places. The absolute minimum is a well-lighted area in front of the garage; one at the main unloading point, if different; another where guests park. Each area should have its own switch, if possible, since they will probably not all be in use at the same time.

A well-lighted area usually requires more than one light; at night, a single light source casts sharp shadows that are annoying at best and can be confusing or deceptive. The lights should be high off the ground, up to about 20 feet, so that glare is not directed into the eyes of approaching drivers. For more information, see *Outdoor Lighting*, p. 2324.

A quarter-circle driveway, on a corner lot, connects the two streets bordering the property and provides direct access to both. The drive is divided in front of the house to form a decorative planting island—and a parking lane.

Crushed stone may be the least expensive paving material, but cost obviously need not detract from beauty. Few concrete or asphalt driveways could be as attractive as the one shown here. Twin head-in parking spaces are conveniently placed near the front entrance to the house, at a 90-degree angle to the driveway. There is a bumper log at the head of each parking space, and each is individually defined by colorful strip plantings along the sides. The blending color of the gravel complements plantings, grass, fence, and house, and forms a neat textured surface. Low steps and entry walk of brick lead to the front door from the special parking spaces and from the main parking area directly in front of the garage. The entire layout—colorful, convenient, practical—provides a generous amount of turnaround space.

Achieve New Utility
And Beauty with Division

A partition is a device that helps you conquer space by dividing it. It can be temporary or permanent. It can look like a solid wall, or it can slide, fold, collapse, or stand free. It can section off part of a room, although without total separation. It can exactly fill your need for privacy, storage, routing of household traffic, or decorative interest.

The most practical function of a partition is to organize distinct but related areas within a single room. For an attractive and convenient place to eat, partition a special dining area from a kitchen or living room. Convert a section of your living room or bedroom into a den, study, or library, making a private retreat for work and relaxation. Establish a separate entertainment, music, game, or hobby center within a family room or living room, custom-planned for your particular requirements. Partitions can add a necessary entryway to a living room, turn a useless alcove into a combination study and storage area, or provide a dressing area for a master bedroom.

In addition to making room for special activities, partitions may also provide the needed extra storage and work space for these activities on either or both sides of itself. Moreover, a partition may conceal a work area such as a home office or laundry center from view of the rest of the house, allowing work in progress to be left undisturbed in its attendant disorder.

Decorate with partitions, adding architectural interest to a plain room or hiding imperfections behind exciting new materials.

Striped fabric stretched on wood frames, supported by poles from floor to ceiling, forms an attractive divider reminiscent of the movable Japanese shoji. The simplicity of the fabric blends well with the pale walls and floor, while the frame adds structural interest to the clean modern lines of the room. The partition sets off the library-music center from the intimate dining area.

A massive chimney partitions the living and informal eating ▶ areas of the family room pictured opposite. The clean lines of the pale yellow brick complement the softer texture of the natural-ash wall paneling and the exposed cedar ceiling. The dining-room side of the chimney serves as a picture wall, and in the conversation area the fireplace shelf serves as a setting for art objects.

Shelf and cabinet partitions

Multipupose partitions offer many advantages for modern living: flexible room division, practical storage and display facilities, and exciting opportunities for decoration. A combination divider might consist of shelves, storage containers, racks, and other useful features designed to meet specific needs.

Open shelves make excellent dividers. They can be mounted in a freestanding frame or suspended on tension poles. Accessible from both sides, such shelves offer good display areas for collections of crystal, sculpture, objets d'art, or exotic plants, and can be specially lighted for effective illumination. Whether wood, metal, glass, or plastic, such partitions have a see-through effect producing an open, airy look that makes a small area seem more spacious.

Modern divider wall units combine open display niches, closed shelves, and concealed storage cabinets in a wide assortment of modular designs. Each module is custom-fitted to its function, and the variety of possible arrangements achieves dramatic results. For maximum flexibility, use separate sections or cubes set in a frame structure braced between the floor and ceiling. These make a permanent-looking divider that is easy to assemble and to change.

Convert a wasted corner into a home library, using a bookcase partition with a closed back, racks, magazine holders, a reading stand, an open niche for a globe, and good direct lighting. Cases for mounted displays protect and exhibit collector's items and can also partition a work area devoted to the pursuit of a hobby. The china hutch for dishes, glassware, and fancy serving pieces, mounted on top of a buffet or cabinet holding silverware, napkins, and other dining necessities, makes an ideal storage-display-buffet divider to separate a dining area from a living room or kitchen.

A freestanding music wall can be built around an upright instrument like a spinet piano or electric organ. Supported by a system of tension

To finish a basement, you may need to build partitions to separate rooms and enclose utilities. First, select the location, considering traffic patterns for activities, allowing room for movable furniture and appliances, and checking overhead clearance to avoid ceiling obstructions. Using straightedge or square, mark lines for floor plate. Next, with a tape measure or plumb, measure and mark the proposed height of the partition. It is easiest to build it across or between joists. When you build under pipes or ducts, use the lowest clearance as the height of the divider. Assemble the sections of the wall on a level floor, then raise them as a unit. Studs are spaced on 16-inch centers, but this can vary as needed. Wedge 2x4 nailers between joists 24 inches apart before raising the section. When section is in place, shim with wedge between top of frame and nailer.

pole units, shelves hold the amplifier, speakers, stereo turntable, tape deck, and other components. Records, tapes, and sheet music can be stored on shelves or in cabinets below.

Similarly, an entertainment center can be constructed using compartments for a television set, games, and bar and snack service. Set off a rumpus area for youngsters or adults with specialized cabinets for playroom equipment: toys and trains; darts and boards; the paddles, cues, and balls for Ping-Pong and pool tables.

Even a closet can succeed as a room divider. A large freestanding closet with access doors on both sides provides plentiful storage for a variety of items. Partition the inside for cubicles, shelves, and hanging racks to fill your storage needs. For protection against moths, line all inside surfaces with red cedar.

Quick-change partitions

Folding partitions, either accordion-folded vinyl or hinged wood panels, afford a room great func-tional flexibility. They can be slid open to serve as walls or closed to expand the room's area. They can partition a temporary guest room in the living room or provide a screen between dining area and kitchen.

Many of these folding partitions, along with the ceiling tracks required for smooth opera-tion and for support, are available ready-made. Such partitions can also be made by the do-it-yourselfer either with wood panels or with heavy fabric stretched on a steel frame. You can build such a partition along the lines of a folding screen; the angled bottom edge will provide adequate stability. If your partition is excep-tionally long or heavy, however, it should have ceiling support.

Sliding screens in the style of the Japanese shoji offer another attractive system of parti-tioning. Again, unless the panels are very short, they will require ceiling tracks.

Partitions offer almost unlimited decorating scope. They can in themselves provide archi-

To secure the wall section, nail upward through the top of frame, wedge, and nailer. On inside cor-ners, overlap double studs. Check the position of the section after the top is secured, then fasten the end stud and the floor plate to the existing wall and floor with a cartridge-powered stud gun. Next, nail the paneling material, such as gypsum wall-board, to the framework. With wallboard, the last hammer blow should dimple the surface to countersink the nailhead. Final-ly, cut the wallboard by scoring the paper cover, then breaking the wallboard over a straight-edge. For accurate corner cut-ting, nail the wallboard in place first, then score and break over the corner stud. To finish surface, fill wallboard joints, including outside and inside corners, with asbestos joint cement, then cover with paper joint tape. Sand with medium (3/0) sandpaper.

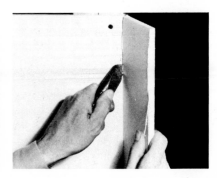

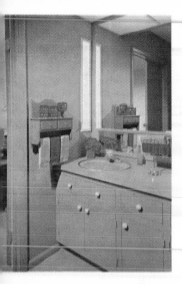

A full partition sections off a part of a large master bedroom to provide visual privacy in a dressing room. The partition also supports a fluorescent fixture to supplement the ceiling light panels. Besides providing a lavatory and generous counter space, the dressing room also provides plenty of storage space—drawers and cabinets below the vanity top and shelves behind mirrored sliding doors. The bedroom carpeting has been extended into the dressing area for plush comfort and continuity of decor, and the bedroom's total restful turquoise and avocado color scheme is used in a new treatment to integrate the multi-purpose area.

tectural interest when constructed of panels, slats, modules, or even pillars. They can provide textural variety with such materials as fabric, wood, glass, wallboard, plastic, metal, brick, or concrete. Style, color, and design may suit any decor from traditional to ultramodern, and can be exchanged for a different atmosphere on the other side of the divider. An informal bookcase and work cabinet that form a home office on

This unusual divider directs traffic from the entry to the ▶ living room, past the dining area which is out of view at the left. It is constructed of cedar boards reaching from floor to ceiling. The boards are spaced on 3-inch centers; small blocks of cedar placed at varying heights space the boards. The vertical thrust of the divider's lines contributes a dynamic counterpoint to the room.

One simple partition cured a great many defects in the living room shown below. Where before both invited guests and unwelcome salesmen were admitted willy-nilly directly into the living room, the partition now provides a sizable entrance hall by sectioning off part of the living room. The partition also provides privacy for anyone using the living room as well as shielding him from drafts.

Partitioning living room and den, this ingenious divider also provides display and storage units flanking the doorway. The wall was sectioned into four major units with ¾-inch particle board. Stereo cabinets are built in at the bottom, and soffits with translucent plastic lighting panels are placed across the top. Adjustable glass shelves hold books and collections.

one side, for example, might be backed with a fancy mirror and wall sconces to make a gracious backdrop for an elegant living room.

Mirrored partitions can make a room seem larger by visually doubling its volume. In addition, their reflective glitter provides imaginative decoration in many traditional and contemporary styles. Fabric-covered panels coordinated with colors and patterns used elsewhere in the partitioned room lend a sense of unity to the decorating scheme. Matching paint or paper covering can achieve a similar effect.

A room divider may seem as solid as a brick wall or as delicate as a filigree railing. A partition built of heavy material—marble, tile, or wood—will lend an illusion of elegant permanence. Latticework and grillwork, on the other hand, allow the passage of light to make exotic or geometric patterns that add to the decorative value. See also *Dividers,* Vol. 7, p. 1198.

The L-shaped partition built within the bedroom above gives the room a more workable plan, privacy for an added dressing room, and, counting both sides of the partition, almost 30 feet of extra wall space. In the dressing room, the partition supports a built-in vanity table and cabinets.

◄ Floor-to-ceiling draperies hung along one side of the living room opposite curtain off an intimate dining alcove. The 4x4 posts, faced with burlap, suggest an archway. Print curtains are lined with solid blue, matching the living room on one side, the dining room on the other.

Lacy fretwork partitions the master bedroom suite shown at right to provide a comfortable sitting room in one corner. The pierced screens, inset in a sturdy frame of wood moldings, permit the passage of both air and light into the windowless sleeping area.

A partitioned partition furnishes a series of niches along one wall of the family room above. The primary partition separates family room and kitchen. The nearest niche, which can be entirely closed with louvered screens, houses a counter that doubles as snack bar and serving buffet. The second niche shelters a cozy corner for reading and conversation. And at the end of the partition, the final niche provides a short corridor linking the family room to the rest of the house. The partition is paneled with walnut.

A room can be functionally partitioned without construction, as the furniture arrangement in the living room at left shows. A large end table and the sofa prohibit circulation along the outside wall and direct all traffic through a narrow channel at one end of the sitting area.

The sweeping architectural lines of this contemporary ▶ divider, meticulously crafted of walnut, pecan, Brazilian rosewood, and other hardwoods, were inspired by the graceful colonnades of Brasilia, capital of Brazil. Sleek molded panels conceal the two hinged doors of the cabinet base. The design's striking simplicity combines modern elegance with timeless significance and beauty.

Master/Guide

Outdoor Entertaining

The reception of guests on a patio or in a yard; the term usually implies the serving of food and drink. For a discussion of the design and equipment of outdoor entertaining centers, see *Outdoor Entertaining*, p. 2307.

Outdoor Lighting

The application of electric light to the illumination of gardens and pathways for purposes of safety and decoration. For a discussion of planning, equipment, and lighting techniques, see *Outdoor Lighting*, p. 2324.

Outdoor Living

A broad term covering a number of family activities pursued on terraces or patios, and including recreation, cooking, and eating. For a discussion of facilities, see *Outdoor Living*, p. 2332.

Outdoor Planting

Flowers and small shrubs suitable for cultivation in beds or in planting boxes used to decorate patios and porches. For a discussion of proper plant selection, as well as of the techniques, tools, and design principles involved in gardening, see *Outdoor Planting*, p. 2346.

Outdoor Play Area

Outdoor area designed, landscaped, and located to accommodate the sports, games, and other entertainments of children. For a discussion of the equipment and treatment of such areas, see *Outdoor Play Areas*, p. 2368.

Outdoor Project

A practical construction and decorating project designed to facilitate home maintenance. For suitable projects, see *Outdoor Projects*, p. 2376.

Outdoor Shade Area

An area carefully cultivated in order to produce shade that will enhance home design as well as increase interior decorating possibilities. For a discussion, see *Outdoor Shade*, p. 2382.

Outing Flannel

A light cotton fabric with a downy nap often used for infants' clothing. Outing flannel is manufactured in white, dyed, and printed goods.

Outrounded

A general term used to describe a flat surface, such as a table or desktop, that has two or four corners formed by an arc rather than by the more conventional right angle. The term can also be applied to furniture that has a facade shape other than that suggested by a square or rectangle, such as the yoke-front console table or commode.

Oval-back Chair

An eighteenth-century English chair with open wooden arms and a back in the shape of an

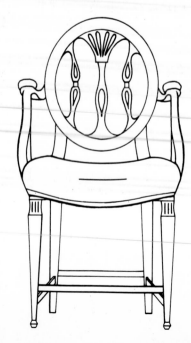

oval, or medallion. The oval often contained a vertical splat and was attached to an upholstered seat by a short hip on either side. In French furniture, a similar chair—known as *le médaillon*—often featured manchettes and an upholstered oval rather than a wooden splat.

Overdoor

A semicircular structure, usually in the form of a window, set over a large door. When formed of glass, the overdoor is similar to the fanlight, except that the mullions (slender bars forming divisions in the glass) are used more decoratively. Elegant and artfully designed overdoors were characteristic of eighteenth-century English domestic architecture.

Finely made blue glass vase from Pompeii. White glass overlay depicts a scene of grape harvesting.

Overhanding

A stitchery technique involving closely sewn short overhand stitches. Overhanding is used to fasten trimming or finishes to the base fabric.

Overlay (or Cameo) Glass

Heavy glass embellished with lightly colored figures or patterns formed in relief against a dark background. To shape the decoration, a layer of dark glass is encased by a layer of lightly tinted glass. The top layer is then, according to the design, ground or cut away in order to reveal the underlying color and to raise the decorative portion into relief. The relief itself may be further modeled in order to enhance its sculptural qualities. Overlay glass is an ancient art form, but it was brought to a high state of development during the nineteenth century, especially in England.

Overmantel Mirror (and Shelves)

A large mirror placed over the mantel shelf. The decorative aspects of the mirror were designed to complement the configuration and mood of the fireplace paneling. During the nineteenth century, the overmantel mirror was appointed with shelves. In some later instances, the shelving displaced the mirror entirely, evolving into an elaborate series of platforms for the display of plate and decorative objects.

Overprint

Term used in textiles to describe the technique of printing one pattern or color over another in order to effect a change in design or color. A similar technique is used in book printing.

Oversailing

A structural device employed in classical and Renaissance architecture in which a row of sculptured brackets was used to support an overhanging cornice. The brackets are known as corbels or consoles. Oversailing was sometimes used as a decorative motif on Renaissance furniture.

Overstuffed

A term used in a general way to refer to fully and puffily upholstered sofas and armchairs. The contours of overstuffed furniture are determined by the amount and kind of stuffing used in the upholstery process. For a discussion of upholstery techniques, see *Upholstery,* Vol. 17.

Ovolo (or Quarter Round)

In classical architecture, the term for a convex molding, either plain or decorated. When modeled with repetitive half-egg motifs separated by slender vertical strips, the molding is known as egg and dart. Molding styles derived from classical architecture were frequently used in designing Renaissance furniture.

Owl Jug

A large, brightly enameled ceramic vase in the shape of an owl. The head is a fitted cover, and, when removed, the jug is used as a drinking cup. In late medieval Germany, owl jugs were given as prizes to the winners of archery contests.

Oxbow (or Yoke-front) Chest

An eighteenth- and nineteenth-century commode (or similar piece) that has a front facade formed by a concave center and convex corners, thus reversing the more conventional serpentine, or bombé, shape.

Oxeye (or Oeil-de-Boeuf) Window (and Mirror)

A round or oval window often found on buildings erected in classical styles. The French name means *eye of the bull,* or bull's-eye. In the eighteenth century, a round or oval convex mirror was a popular form of girandole. It was usually set in a gilded frame with a single candle fixture on either side.

Oxeye windows in the seventeenth-century castle of the Order of the Teutonic Knights; Ellington, Germany.

Oxhorn Cup

A medieval drinking cup constructed from the horn of an ox. The horn was hollowed out and then frequently mounted in metal. The term is also applied to metal cups shaped in the form of a horn.

Oyster, Daniel (1764-1845)

A noted American clock designer who worked in Pennsylvania. Oyster is best known for his unusually fine tall case clocks.

Oyster Grain (and Oystering)

The distinctive irregular concentric circles appearing in side or diagonal cuts of walnut and laburnum saplings. The configuration resembles the inside of an oyster shell. Oystering, a mode of decorating furniture with various arrangements of these pieces, was popular in England during the reigns of Charles II and of William and Mary.

Ozier Pattern

An openwork border modeled in relief to simulate basket weaving. It was first introduced in German ceramics.

Ozone Fading

A textile term used to refer to the tendency of acetate fabrics to change color when adversely affected by atmospheric conditions.

Padauk (or Madou)

A hard, lustrous wood similar to rosewood, which ranges in color from pink to brown. The wood is native to Asia, Africa, and South America. It became popular with French *ébénistes* during the eighteenth century, particularly for decorative purposes.

Padding

In textiles, the process (and the machine required to implement it) often used in extensive production to apply dyestuffs to fabrics.

Pad (and Cushioned Pad) Foot

A graceful oval foot, of varying form, which often terminated the cabriole leg during the Queen Anne period. The varieties of pad foot include the club foot (blunt and thick), the drake foot (cloven into three gently pointed parts), the slipper foot (a pointed oval), and the snake foot (long, rounded, with the oval almost resting on the floor). When a small disk is used to support and protect the pad, the foot is then known as a *cushioned* pad foot.

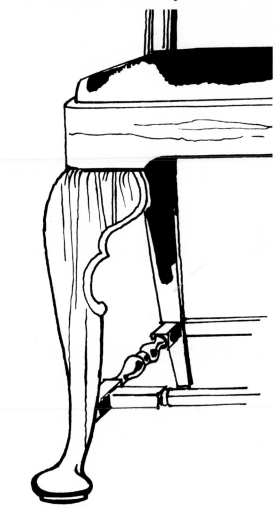

Paduasoy

Heavy corded silk fabric used since the Renaissance for ceremonial vestments and for wall hangings. The name is a sobriquet for *soie de Padua* in recognition of the eminence of Italian (and especially Paduan) versions of this silk.

Pagoda

An elaborate polygonal tower characteristic of Chinese religious architecture. The tower comprises a series of tiers that sweep out and up

Exquisite "Pagoda of Flowers;" Canton, China. Pagodas are memorials that symbolize Buddhist cosmology.

from the central structure, each suggestive of the shape of the roof that crowns the tower. During the eighteenth-century chinoiserie vogue, the graceful roof and tower shapes were transformed into decorative bed canopies and cabinet pediments.

Paine, James (1725-89)

An English architect and designer who worked in the Georgian neoclassic style. Paine is noted especially for his ornamental treatment of walls and ceilings.

Paint

A mixture of pigment with a suitable liquid base, used to coat interior and exterior surfaces for both protection and decoration. For a discussion of paints and their applications, see *Paints and Painting,* p. 2392.

Paisley

The name given to a distinctive pattern appearing on woven or printed fabrics, originally made in Paisley, Scotland. The pattern, derived from the sinuous and complex motifs of Persia (such as those found on Persian rugs), is character-

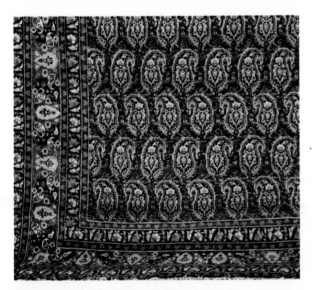

Persian rugs, such as this one from Heriz, Iran, were the original inspiration for paisley designs.

ized by large, brightly colored scroll forms. Fabrics with paisley patterns are popular for clothing, draperies, and decorative items.

Paktong

A metal alloy composed of copper, nickel, and zinc imported from the Orient during the eighteenth century and used in the manufacture of fireplace tools and other items. It was used in lieu of silver and to imitate it. Paktong is sometimes called "German silver," although the latter is an alloy with a different proportion of the same components.

Palampore

Cotton fabric, originally made in East India, decorated with hand-painted motifs, most characteristically the "tree of life," a stylized tree with interlacing branches, foliage, and birds. This fabric, first imported to Europe during the seventeenth century, was often used for bedcovers and decorative hangings.

Palanquin

A vehicle designed to convey one person. The palanquin, common during the seventeenth century, was shaped like a lightly scaled wardrobe. It had a windowed door on the front, a seat within, and windows on either side. Poles, attached on either side and projecting before and behind, allowed the palanquin to be carried by four bearers, two in front and two in back.

Pale Colors

A term broadly applied to colors that have a low intensity, or chroma. Pale colors are, in this respect, related to neutral colors. For a discussion of pale colors and related matters, see *Color,* Vol. 5, p. 842.

Palissy, Bernard (c.1510-90)

A French potter, enamelist, and chemist renowned for his skill in using glazes. Palissy is also known as the founder of a style of rendering natural objects which has persisted in French

Jewel-toned "La Fécondité" plate, attributed to Bernard Palissy: glazed earthenware with molded relief.

ceramics since his time. Palissy ware was produced until the seventeenth century.

Palladio, Andrea (1518-80)

An Italian architect and scholar who was responsible for the revival of an accurate classic Roman architectural style. His buildings are renowned for their stateliness, vigor, and careful proportions. Palladio's architectural achievements and books on design, particularly *I quattro libri dell'architettura,* had an enormous influence on styles throughout Europe and America. Palladian style was particularly popular in England, where it was first introduced by Inigo Jones, although it was used most extensively during the eighteenth century. In America, Thomas Jefferson was one of the chief proponents of Palladianism; the Federalist style was one of its offshoots.

Palmette Motif

A highly stylized palm leaf in a semicircular form resembling the fan motif. The palmette motif was a common decoration on ancient Egyptian furniture.

Palm Motif

An ancient stylized decorative motif based on the palm tree, particularly its bouquet of fountainlike fronds. In ancient Egypt, the palm motif was a common form of column capital.

Interior of Church of San Giorgio Maggiore demonstrates Palladio's unique adaptation of classical architecture.

Panached

In textiles, used to refer to bizarre or complex patterns, often of variegated stripes.

Panchetto

A wooden side chair of distinctive design, a specialty of Italian Renaissance cabinetry. The panchetto had three splayed legs, an oval or polygonal seat, no arms, and a simple, often fan-shaped, back resembling a back splat without any framing structure. The panchetto is similar to the *sgabello,* but it is less refined in construction and decoration. Both the panchetto and the *sgabello* are popular furnishings in contemporary Mediterranean styles.

Panel (and Paneling)

A framed surface forming part of another and larger surface. Panels are of three general kinds, depending upon the relationship of the surface to the framing molding. The surface may be sunk below the molding (sunken panel), raised above the molding (bolection panel), or both surface and molding may be flush with the area upon which the panel appears (painted or inlaid panels). The molding, resembling a picture frame, and the surface, resembling a picture, are susceptible to a variety of decorative treatments. For a discussion of the types and of the decorative possibilities of panels, see *Paneling,* p. 2432.

Panel-back (or Wainscot) Chair

A large Elizabethan oak armchair with an unusually tall back adorned with a crested rail and closed by panels. The chair, heavy and handsomely carved, had turned legs and stretcher bars. In some instances, the chair back

Intricately ornamented and gilded paneling in the music room of the eighteenth-century Hotel de Lauzun, Paris.

was topped by a flat and carved cornice. Although the styles varied, the panel-back chair, until the end of the seventeenth century, remained one of the most important chairs among English furnishings. The alternate name, wainscot chair, derives from the fact that oak wall paneling was known as wainscoting.

Panetiere

A small, ornate French-provincial cabinet used for storing bread. Particularly charming examples survive from the seventeenth century. These have a small central door, with the remaining front facade and sides formed by turned spindles open to provide proper ventilation. Often carved or painted in rococo style, they sat upon the short, stubby cabriole legs characteristic of provincial furniture. For a discussion of the characteristics of French-provincial styles, see *Furniture Styles,* Vol. 9, p. 1626.

Panne

The textile term for a pile fabric, such as silk, satin, or velvet, that has been specially finished in order to produce a high luster. The name is derived from the French word for "plush."

Panoply

An ornamental motif composed of armorial elements, weapons, and festooned fabrics arranged in a balanced manner against a wall as a decoration. The term is also applied to this motif when used in paintings or tapestries.

Pantries

A small area associated with the kitchen, but sometimes separate or set off from it, intended for the storage of staple foods, canned goods, and seldom-used cooking utensils. Some perishables may also be stored there. For a discussion of the organization and equipping of such areas, see *Pantries,* p. 2446.

Papelera

A rectangular and portable Spanish Renaissance document cabinet. The papelera contained small door-closed units and rows of drawers. Handsomely carved, it usually rested upon a trestle-table stand. Although similar to the *vargueno,* one of the most characteristic of Spanish Renaissance writing cabinets, the papelera lacked a drop front and therefore could not serve as a desk.

Paper Cloth

Cloth manufactured from yarns derived from paper fibers. Paper cloth, although it did not wear well, was first used by the Germans for clothing during World War I. It has practical uses for articles other than clothing.

Paper Projects

The use of paper to create decorative as well as useful accessories. For a discussion of the techniques and applications of this ancient art, see *Paper Projects,* p. 2252.

Paperweight

A small and heavy weight of glass, metal, stone, marble, etc., originally designed as a desk furnishing to keep papers from scattering. The first paperweights were made in France early in the nineteenth century, of highly decorative glass, and were of such remarkable artistry and reflected such technical skill that they now constitute prizes for professional collectors and museums. Most often the shape was polygonal or oval and slightly flattened at the base. The glass, clear or cut into prisms, enclosed colored glass flowers, birds, insects, animals, portraits, or fluid designs in millefiori, filigree, or latticinio glass. The finest French paperweights were made at Baccarat, St. Louis, and Clichy.

Papier-mache

Paper, cut into strips, mixed with glue and chalk (or other ingredients that can affect color or texture), then mashed to a pulpy consistency suitable for working, somewhat in the manner of plaster or clay, into ornaments, accessories, and small pieces of furniture. Although the technique derives from the ancient Near East, it was first practiced widely in France during the eighteenth century, later becoming very popular in England, especially during the Victorian period. Once in a workable condition, the mashed paper is molded and let dry, resulting in a surprisingly sturdy and durable substance. Papier-mâché articles were often japanned, inlaid, or painted. Popular Victorian papier-mâché items included fancy boxes, clock cases, mirror ornaments, fire screens, and side chairs.

Papiers Colle

French term (from the verb *coller,* to glue) for the modern technique of developing pictorial images by pasting common articles, such as tiny boxes, ticket stubs, strings, and paper, onto a canvas, often with a ludicrous or satirical effect. It is another name for collage.

"Bottle of Suze," Picasso, papier collé. This medium is a subcategory of collage invented by Braque and Picasso.

Papillon, Jean (1661-1723)

A noted French wallpaper designer and manufacturer. Papillon was the first to devise wallpaper designs in such a manner that sections could be matched at the seams.

Paraments

Heavy figured fabrics, such as brocades and damasks, often woven with gold and silver threads and used in ceremonial clothing and ecclesiastical hangings.

Parapet

In Gothic architecture, a wall (often provided with apertures for unexposed reconnaissance) placed around a large balcony or the walkway of a circular tower. In Renaissance architecture, the parapet was the portion of the facade that extended above the roof line. This structure was often formed by a balustrade adorned with statuary placed at regular intervals.

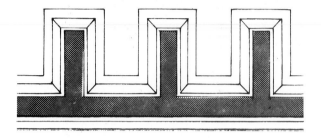

Parcel Gilding

A form of gilding that involves only selected portions of furniture or its ornamentation. Parcel gilding, popular during the rococo period, was often employed on painted furniture. The term is also used in metalworking, where it is applied to silver or other metals that have been partially gilded.

Gilded bronze cabinet mount. An example of parcel gilding during rococo period.

Pargework (or Pargeting)

In interior design, the technique of decorative plasterwork, with the designs executed either in relief or indented, used primarily for the ornamentation of walls and ceilings. Pargework was also employed to simulate structural members such as ceiling ribs or supporting columns.

Grotesques from the Villa Madama, Rome. Examples of sixteenth-century stucco pargework.

Parian Ware

Hard-paste nineteenth-century English porcelain that resembled Parian marble (cream-colored marble from the island of Paros in the Cyclades). Typical Parian ware included statuettes, vases, bibelots, and tablewares. American Parian ware, made in Bennington, Vermont, was known as statuary ware.

Parking Area

Space designed for the convenient temporary accommodation of automobiles. For a detailed

Bureau of Louis XV, an eighteenth-century masterpiece of bronze-doré and parquetry.

discussion of the location, construction, and maintenance of such areas, see *Parking and Driveways,* p. 2260.

Parliament Clock

An inexpensive wooden eighteenth-century English wall clock, usually found in inns. The parliament clock derived its name from the fact that an act of the English parliament in 1797 (repealed in 1798) levied a tax on all clocks. In anticipation of the increased cost of clocks, innkeepers provided their accommodations with inexpensive wooden varieties. The name was later applied to any inexpensive clock situated in a public place.

Parquet Floor

A hardwood floor formed of small pieces of wood inlaid to form a geometric pattern. Parquet floors of unique elegance were devised in France and England during the eighteenth century. For a discussion of parquet floors, see *Floors and Floor Coverings,* Vol. 8, p. 1418.

Parquetry

The art of inlaying on furniture (and floors) small pieces of wood contrasting in color or texture in order to form geometric patterns. Although parquetry is related to marquetry, parquetry refers specifically to the creation of geometric patterns. Furniture with parquet decoration was extremely popular during the reign of Louis XV.

Partition

An interior divider used to separate one room or area from another. Technically it is not a wall because it bears no structural load. For a discussion of how and where to erect partitions, see *Partitions,* p. 2472.

Partridge Wood

A South American hardwood with grain that suggests feathers. Partridge wood was used during the seventeenth and eighteenth centuries for both inlays and cabinetwork. Its color is reddish and mottled.